The Tongue-Tied American

Previous Books by Author

The Politics of World Hunger
(with Arthur Simon)

Lincoln's Preparation for Greatness

Lovejoy: Martyr to Freedom

THE
TONGUE-TIED
AMERICAN

Confronting the Foreign Language Crisis

by Paul Simon

CONTINUUM · New York

1980
The Continuum Publishing Corporation
815 Second Avenue, New York, N.Y. 10017

Library of Congress Cataloging in Publication Data

Simon, Paul, 1928-   The tongue-tied American.
Includes bibliographical references.
1. Languages, Modern—Study and teaching—United
States. I. Title.
PB38.U6S5   407'.073   80-17709   ISBN 0-8264-0022-1

To Jeanne

Contents

Preface

This book is not written by a language expert, nor is it addressed primarily to language experts. My hope is that it will reach much beyond that limited audience.

I am concerned about what is happening in my country and I want to share that concern with others who are serious about the course and destiny of our nation.

During my high school and college years I received a smattering of foreign language exposure, more than most American students, but by no gauge an adequate exposure. During thirteen months in the U.S. Army in Germany, I furthered that language knowledge, and travels since that time have increased my appetite for language skills, more than my abilities.

I have often sensed my own inadequacies in languages, and the inadequacies of most Americans. And I have seen what that inadequacy has cost us as a nation.

I am grateful to many who have directly and indirectly assisted me on this project: my colleagues on the President's Commission on Foreign Language and International Studies, who added to my knowledge; and to these individuals who took time to read and criticize my manuscript: Marta Bret of the University of North Carolina at Charlotte; Richard Brod of the Modern Language Association; Barbara B. Burn of the University of Massachusetts at Amherst; Nan Bell, assistant with the President's Commission; Rose Hayden, with the U.S. International Communications Agency; Martin Marty, historian and theologian at the University of Chicago; John Rassias of Dartmouth College; C. Edward Scebold and W. D. Sims-Gunzenhauser of the American Council on the Teaching of Foreign Languages; S. Frederick Starr of the Kennan Institute of Soviet Studies at the Smithsonian; George Vaught of Appalachian State University; Judith Wagner, a subcommittee staff director for the House Education and Labor Committee; and my brother, Arthur, author and executive director of Bread for the World. Sylvia Corbin typed the final draft and Dianne Cregger the preliminary drafts. Joe Johnson helped on footnotes. Jeannette Hopkins, my editor, has been thorough and patient. My staff, particularly Vicki Otten and Ray Johnsen, did not complain when I let some other work accumulate to work on this manuscript. The title is taken from a *New York Times* editorial caption.

The reader must judge whether I have dealt adequately with a matter which has gone almost unnoticed, but is of extreme importance to the nation's future. My hope is that any deficiencies of the edited book will be more than matched by the overpowering facts that assault us, and are recounted in the pages ahead.

Paul Simon

Introduction

"The Land of the Monolingual"

The United States can be characterized as the home of the brave, and the land of the monolingual.

—Rose Lee Hayden [1]

There was a time when foreign policy was king. For a generation after World War II, Americans told Mr. Gallup that foreign policy was their major concern. Presidential candidates argued about Moscow, Peking, even Quemoy and Matsu. Money poured into university research centers for the study of Communism, underdeveloped countries and nuclear strategy. Newspapers opened expensive overseas bureaus and foreign leaders appeared on the covers of new magazines. All that has changed.

—Editorial, *New York Times* [2]

We should erect a sign at each port of entry into the United States:

—WELCOME TO THE UNITED STATES—
WE CANNOT SPEAK YOUR LANGUAGE

At a time when the national need dictates that we should be increasing the exposure of our citizens to other languages and cultures, that exposure is declining. Cultural isolation is a luxury the United States can no longer afford, but we are nevertheless culturally isolated.

Here are some examples of our present situation:

• Of those who graduate from public high school today, fewer than 4 percent have more than two years of a foreign language. By comparison, France (which we sometimes criticize for cultural isolation or arrogance) requires all students to take at least four years of a foreign language starting in the sixth grade. In 1974 there were one-half million fewer United States high school students enrolled in foreign languages than in 1968, despite the growth in total student enrollment during those years. Of 22,737 secondary schools in the nation, 4,344 do not teach any foreign language, and the number of schools that do teach foreign languages is declining.

• In 1915, 36 percent of American students in high school were studying modern foreign languages. In 1976, the most recent year for which statistics are available, the most reliable figure is 17.9 percent, and declining. Many thoughtful citizens share Stanford University's concern: "There is an increasing number of secondary schools, indeed entire school districts, where even the most capable students will have taken little or no foreign language since the ninth grade." [3]

• After Sputnik's ascent in 1957 there was a flurry of interest in teaching languages in the elementary schools. Foreign language teaching at the elementary level now reaches only a fraction of 1 percent of our students, and even that is declining, despite the fact that most authorities agree that the elementary grades are the best time to begin to learn a foreign language.

• The United States continues to be the only nation where you can graduate from college without having had one year of a foreign language during any of the twelve years of schooling. It is even possible to earn a doctorate here without studying any foreign language.

• Forty-four percent fewer students enrolled in college foreign-language programs between 1963 and 1974, despite the fact that during that same period the nation became much more dependent upon exports for jobs.

• One-fifth of the nation's two-year colleges offer no foreign language. (For two years [1973 and 1974] I taught at Sangamon State University in Illinois, in most respects a fine school. But not a single foreign language course is taught there.) By contrast, most of the developed nations—and many of the developing nations—offer every elementary school student the chance to learn a foreign language.

• In 1915, 85 percent of the nation's colleges required that a student pass a competency test in a foreign language before he or she could enter. As of 1975, only 10 percent of the nation's colleges or universities even required that the school record show that the student had taken a foreign language.

• A 1973 survey revealed that only 5 percent of those graduating to become teachers had taken any course that exposed them to the culture of another country or to international politics.

• In a survey of all Indiana schools, kindergarten through college, administrators, asked how many new foreign language teachers they would need in the next five years due to retirements, expanded programs, or changes in programs, replied: seven teachers for five years for the whole state. That means more steps backwards in Indiana. (Dr. Rose Hayden, a scholar of the language scene, suggested tongue-in-cheek that language teachers should be put on the endangered species list.)

• A 1977 Indiana survey of changes in high school enrollments from the 1971–72 school year showed that, despite larger enrollments, Spanish was down 8.9 percent; French, 22.3 percent; German, 6.5 percent; Latin, 52.2 percent; and Russian, 67.2 percent.

• Because of inflation, California-spawned Proposition 13

fever, and declining enrollments, schools are in a financial squeeze. Language programs often take the brunt, as a *Washington Post* editorial indicated about District of Columbia schools: "On the very morning teachers were reporting back to work last week—70 tenured teachers, including two-thirds of all the foreign language teachers in the elementary system, two of whom have 17 years experience—were told they won't have jobs after the end of this month." [4]

• Of the eleven million U.S. students seeking graduate and undergraduate degrees, fewer than 1 percent are studying the languages used by three-fourths of the world's population, and only a small number of that small number will ever achieve a reasonable degree of competence. For example, there are 300 million people who speak Hindi, but fewer than 300 Americans are studying that language.

• Because knowledge of foreign languages has diminished so substantially, the State Department no longer requires any background in another language as a condition of entry into the Foreign Service.

• The federal government has established a category in some jobs labeled "language essential," yet a recent federal report shows more than one-third of these not satisfactorily filled. In some languages—Arabic, for example—well over half of "language essential" jobs are not filled by linguists.

• Because of our rich ethnic mix, the United States is home to millions whose first language is not English. One of every fifty Americans is foreign-born. We are the fourth largest Spanish-speaking country in the world. Yet almost nothing is being done to preserve the language skills we have or to use this rich linguistic resource to train people in the use of a language other than English.

And even this array of illustrations and statistics can be deceptive, for along with the problem of quantity, of numbers, there is also a serious problem of quality. Heywood Broun said that he had taken beginners' French in school but when he got to Paris he discovered that no one there spoke beginners' French. Tests show that only 17 percent of those who study a foreign language wholly within the United States can speak, write, or read the language with ease; of those who have studied abroad, 63 percent can speak, write, or read with ease.

Because of this language gap the loss to the nation's cultural life is inestimable. We are linguistically malnourished. Yet never in history has there been one nation with such a variety of ethnic and language backgrounds.

This language inattention threatens our national security interests; the adverse impact on the nation's economy is immense. At a White House breakfast for some members of Congress, Federal Reserve Board Chairman William Miller estimated that more than one-ninth of the nation's inflation in 1978 had been caused by the adverse balance of trade between the U.S. and other nations—in particular, Japan—and the subsequent slippage in the value of the dollar.

A few days after the White House breakfast, I flipped through the *Congressional Record* to find Senator S. I. Hayakawa of California discussing the adverse U.S. balance of trade with Japan. He pointed out that in New York City there are approximately 10,000 Japanese salesmen—all of whom speak English—while in all of Japan there are approximately 1,000 American salesmen, few of whom speak Japanese. Who do you think sells more? Those figures are not precise; but the huge disparity is not disputed.

A senior Japanese leader made the same point to a University of Maryland official:

> Your nation has experienced difficulties in balance of payments; your nation now faces severe competition in world markets. . . . Why can your continuing education not teach foreign languages and customs and cultures of the countries where they may be traveling and working? Our Japanese

business people study the language, the customs and cultures of the United States, Canada, Western Europe and Southeast Asia, and we have been extremely successful in selling our manufactured goods abroad because we understand the people and their needs. Our people do not operate through interpreters. Our representatives speak the language of the host country and they know it well—and also the customs. Recently I read that there has been a serious drop of enrollments in most foreign language courses in the United States. . . . Your people must give greater consideration to the study of languages and customs of foreign lands or you will lose in the competitive world markets.[5]

For two decades after World War II the United States remained dominant economically as it once was militarily. Military dominance diminished dramatically when the Soviets exploded a nuclear weapon; in an instant the world's military balance had shifted. The Soviet's first space flight, dubbed Sputnik, had military implications.

But in the world of economics no bombs exploded and no Sputniks ascended. We sold to countries who came to us. We sent a few sales representatives abroad, but our products were in demand; if someone could not speak English, we secured an interpreter or denied that potential customer the "privilege" of buying from us. The nearest thing to a nuclear bomb or a Sputnik in the economic field was the 1973 oil embargo by the Arab nations. Days of dollar dominance and easy sales were over. Our response to our decline in economic power has been anemic or blundering. We have not responded as we did to Sputnik, with an accelerated program of our own.

When General Motors put out its Chevrolet Nova, apparently no one thought of foreign sales. *Nova* when spoken as two words in Spanish means, "It doesn't go." Not surprisingly, sales were few in Puerto Rico and Latin America. With the name hastily changed to *Caribe,* the car sold well. When Parker Pen put on a sales campaign in South America, a less-than-accurate Spanish translation promised buyers that the new ink used in the pen would prevent unwanted pregnancies.

Our nation's position in the field of security changed more dramatically, but there, too, we have been learning our lessons slowly. The obvious responses, such as increasing the military budget, flowed easily. After Sputnik, we passed a measure, significantly entitled the National Defense Education Act, which for a few years boosted our interest in other languages and cultures. Had the word *defense* not been in the title, the measure might never have cleared Congress. The nobly conceived International Education Act of 1964, passed almost unanimously by Congress and signed by the President, has yet to receive its first penny of funding.

While it continues to be relatively easy to get appropriations for bombers and submarines and nuclear weapons, we move much less swiftly, if at all, on measures that contribute to real security—a world of adequate communications and cultural understanding, which together could eliminate, or drastically reduce, the need for those bombers and submarines and nuclear weapons. In 1977, Navy Lieutenant Howell Conway Zeigler, assigned as a UN military observer in the Middle East, averted a confrontation by speaking to both sides in Hebrew and Arabic. But how few we have encouraged to develop that type of knowledge.

Any serious discussion of security involves our relationship with the other superpower, the Soviet Union. Although that relationship has had many ups and downs, we cannot forget that the Soviet Union and the United States together possess enough nuclear warheads to destroy every person on the face of the earth many times over. One military official told me a few years ago that the figure is 22 times, while one French authority writes that humanity can destroy itself 690 times. Where the truth rests I hope we do not need to determine, but strengthened understanding between our nations is of critical (the right word) importance.

How are we responding to this overwhelming need for understanding? Today there are more teachers of English in the USSR than there are students of Russian in the United States. In Illinois in the last six years the number of students of Russian in our public schools declined 68 percent. In the nation's two-year community colleges Russian language studies declined 12 percent in the last three years, and the absolute figures are even worse: Of four million community college students, 1,723 were enrolled in a Russian course in 1975 and 1,511 in 1977–78. In four-year colleges and universities and graduate schools the percentage of students enrolled in Russian language courses dropped 14 percent between 1974 and 1977. Fifty-two fewer universities today offer courses in the Russian language than offered them in 1974. (Interestingly, 100 fewer collegiate institutions offer the increasingly important commercial language of German than offered it in 1974.)

It is not uncommon that when our nation must formally or informally engage in dialogue and bargaining at meetings with the Soviets, the Chinese, and others, we are dependent on interpreters provided by the other side. And even if we provide our own, the other side usually has people in its delegations who understand English and can take advantage of the time of translation to calculate a response. Lacking language skills, we lose this small advantage in tough bargaining sessions.

Everyone remembers when the Soviet leader Nikita Khrushchev told us, "We will bury you." Everyone remembers wrong. The correct translation is, "We will survive you." Although neither statement is pleasant to hear, the one we thought we heard is substantially more ominous sounding than what was actually said. Such nuances make a substantial difference in anger and misunderstandings. When President Jimmy Carter visited Poland, the world guffawed at the translation errors. President Carter's wish to "learn your opinions and understand your desires for the future" came out "I desire the Poles carnally." It caused embarrassment to the President and to our country. Wrong translations between potential enemies, however, can lead to difficulties much more serious than minor embarrassments.

Vietnam and the Middle East have taught us that our security position is not solely a matter of dealing with the Warsaw Pact countries or the giants among the nations. Before our heavy intervention in Vietnam, fewer than five American-born experts on Vietnam, Cambodia, or Laos—in all of our universities and the State Department combined—could speak with ease one of the languages of that area. We were almost completely reliant on the French government for our information, and France was prodding us to assume some of the burden she wanted to shed.

What if—a big if—we had had in our nation at that point a mere twenty Americans who spoke Vietnamese fluently, who understood their culture, aspirations, and political history? Maybe, just maybe, we would have avoided that conflict. Ironically, although Vietnam is now the third most populous Communist nation, after China and the Soviet Union, the latest figures show that only twenty-nine persons in our country are enrolled in a course to study the Vietnamese language.

We cannot rerun history, but we can profit by it. And unless we soon learn the importance of establishing better communication with the countries whose names we do not now even recognize, those nations' names will erupt in unhappy headlines in our newspapers, and their affairs will invade our television sets in living color. The alternative to understanding and communicating today is not isolation. It is chaos. That chaos at worst could destroy civilization as we now know it. At best we would experience drastic changes for the worse in our quality of life.

The problem of linguistic isolation coincides with cultural isolation.

A UNESCO survey of 100 nations and their television offerings showed the United States last among the 100 nations in the amount of television time devoted to international items. United States newspapers and radio and television outlets have fewer American staff correspondents abroad today than at any time since World War II. The majority of American newspapers print fewer than three columns of foreign news weekly. A 1974 national survey asked eighth graders: Who is president of Egypt, Anwar Sadat or Golda Meir? A majority selected Golda Meir.

Half a century ago Alfred North Whitehead wrote, "It is the business of the future to be dangerous." We can diminish the danger if we act promptly and wisely. If we act, we can achieve a minor cultural revolution.

The question is not one of national resources. The question is one of national will.

· 1 ·

Americanization Has Its Weaknesses

I consider it the paramount duty of public schools, apart from the educational knowledge to be instilled into our pupils, to form American citizens of them . . . obliterating from the very earliest moment all the distinguishing foreign characteristics and traits, which the beginners may bring with them, as obstructive, warring, and irritating elements.

—Commissioner of the Common Schools
of New York City, 1896 [1]

It is impossible to understand why millions of people . . . must learn two or three foreign languages only a fraction of which they can make use of later and hence most of them forget entirely; for a hundred thousand pupils who learn French, for example, barely two thousand will have a serious use for this knowledge later, while ninety-eight thousand . . . will not find themselves in a position to make practical use of what they once learned. They have . . . devoted thousands of hours to a subject which later is without value and meaning for them. . . . So in reality, because of the two thousand people for whom the knowledge of this language is profitable, ninety-eight thousand must be tormented for nothing and made to sacrifice valuable time.

Adolf Hitler, *Mein Kampf* [2]

There is more than one reason for the lack of emphasis on foreign languages in the United States, but one word,

Americanization, explains a major part of it. That word speaks to this nation's strength and to its weakness.

The United States is the greatest amalgam of people of any single nation. The blending of our backgrounds into both a national culture and a diversity of cultures has not always been a smooth process, not always free of difficulty, but for all its minuses, on balance it has been a tremendous plus for the United States, and an example to other nations.

This Americanization process encouraged Italian, German, Armenian, Japanese, Nigerian, and other immigrants to be "American" in their attitude, culture, and citizenship. A heavily accented English, or strange clothing, or habits that did not fit completely into this new world were "deficiencies" they wanted their children to avoid. Their children went to school to become Americans. To promote this transition, the parents sometimes refused to speak their native tongue around the children; and the children were sometimes embarrassed if they did, and demanded that they speak in English. The last thing most of these parents wanted their children to learn in school was a foreign language. If someone asks the son of Italian immigrants if he speaks Italian, he will often deny it.

To speak another language has been a matter of shame, not of pride. Even third, fourth, and fifth generation Americans are caught in this. There is no sense that they have a resource, important to them personally and important to the nation. So we have this unusual, deep-seated phenomenon: a historical cultural barrier to the learning of another language in a land of great ethnic diversity.

Another reason for our present dilemma is our history of local control of the schools. In almost all other nations, education curriculum and policy are determined at the national level. Local control in the United States applies to hiring teachers and administrators; it applies to building the physical facilities—and it applies to shaping curriculum. There are

50,000 school districts in the fifty states. And no President of the United States, no U.S. Secretary of Education, and no member of the U.S. Senate or House of Representatives can tell even the smallest elementary school in the nation that its curriculum must include any subject.

There have been times when a national need, or national passion, has influenced the curriculum nationwide. During World War I, when anti-German feeling was high, German language teaching virtually disappeared from schools all over the nation. After Sputnik's ascent in 1957, there was a sudden thrust forward in the teaching of sciences, and, to a lesser extent, foreign languages. When there has been a perceived national need, ways to encourage curriculum change have emerged. When we have wanted change, a financial "carrot" has been available to bring education more into line with national needs. A good example is the Smith-Hughes Act, which established a federal subsidy of agricultural education and home economics. Soon after the passage, virtually every high school in the nation could offer these courses.

Foreign language study has been on a roller coaster, but unfortunately the general trend is more down than up. In 1979, approximately 17 percent of all high school students had studied a modern foreign language, a slightly smaller percentage than in 1890. But there is one major difference—in 1890, more than half of all high school students took Latin. Today, fewer than 1 percent study Latin or ancient Greek. The Modern Language Association of America was established in 1883 because scholars found that the study of Latin and ancient Greek had almost completely squeezed out modern language study at both the high school and collegiate levels.

While language study appeared early in our history—missionaries taught French to the Indians as early as 1604—modern languages have usually been taught as "extras," things that enriched the student but had no part in the heart of the curriculum.

Language teaching followed the ethnic background of a community. One source notes that in 1895, nationally there were at least 3,000 elementary pupils enrolled in French classes and 23,000 in German classes, reflecting the immigrant background of the students. These students (and their parents) resisted the general trend toward abandonment of national heritage. The high point in percentages of high school students studying a foreign language appears to have been reached shortly before World War I. With the arrival of World War I, attempts to exclude "foreign" elements from the curriculum had great popular appeal. German, in particular, suffered. By 1922, the number of students who studied German had declined by 98 percent from 1915 levels. Some states attempted to ban the teaching of all foreign languages. Despite that, before World War II, 36 percent of high school students studied a modern foreign language.

During World War II, the national defense establishment found itself in desperate need of linguists. The academic community could not meet the need. Not only had the declining numbers of students resulted in a smaller academic base for foreign language study, but the skills developed were geared more to reading than to the practical needs of the nation's defense leaders. The War Department was compelled to move into the field of foreign language teaching quickly, with programs that differed drastically from the conventional academic approach. But after the war and by the time of Sputnik, foreign language enrollment had dropped to 20 percent; the Soviet space enterprise boosted enrollment up to approximately 24 percent. It was a brief respite. The percentage has gone downhill since that time, reaching an all-time low of less than 17 percent in 1979.

An additional factor militating against national curriculum priorities emerged during the Vietnam era. Students assumed near control of college curricula. American campuses came close to resembling battlegrounds with the violent eruptions at Kent State University in Ohio and Jackson in Mississippi as the tragic climax to this period. On dozens of campuses, rebellious students occupied the president's office, or a dean's office. The slightest provocation sometimes erupted in chaos in the streets. Buildings were burned. Even campuses where violence did not erupt were affected by the turmoil elsewhere.

The curriculum became one of the most vulnerable pressure points. Students wanted fewer requirements for admission and for graduation. And part of the national reaction to Vietnam was an inward movement. Many school administrators, sensing the mood of the times and eager to be among the survivors, found it all too convenient to drop foreign language requirements.

The government nevertheless has been able to exert some influence on foreign language study. A series of government programs has indirectly—and sometimes directly—fostered greater interest in foreign languages. Dr. Rose L. Hayden compiled a list of federal agency programs involved in international education for the American Council on Education; it turned out to be a seventy-six-page document. Unplanned and uncoordinated, these federal programs fill the needs and objectives of the separate agencies. While language requirements are not a part of most of these programs, some do have requirements such as: "Language proficiency sufficient to carry out the proposed study." Each of the programs has a fairly narrow focus, but all result secondarily in a greater appreciation for another culture. Not until I read Dr. Hayden's compilation did I know that there is a Transportation Research Activities Overseas Program operated by the Department of Transportation. Although most of these programs evolved because of the perceived needs and missions of the various agencies, not because of any attempt to satisfy a national desire for greater cultural understanding, exchange, and communication, the result no doubt includes such communication.

By far the biggest federal program in the nation's history has been the National Defense Education Act passed in 1958. That act aimed at meeting "the present national education emergency." Title III of the law authorized payments to state educational agencies to stimulate instruction in a variety of academic subjects, including foreign languages. Close to $100 million has been made available to states, in declining amounts, under this law. But the programs under the 1958 act that helped elementary and high school language programs were few and meagerly financed. Title VI supports graduate and undergraduate foreign studies and language development programs. Title VI programs included institutes for language study, to improve the skills of foreign language teachers; approximately 50,000 teachers increased their skills through this program. This portion of Title VI has not been funded since 1973, but in the course of accumulating background for this book I have come across many teachers who mark their involvement in a language institute as most significant, the point at which their language-teaching skills improved markedly. Another portion of this program, which has also been phased out, funded more than 20,000 electronic language-teaching systems in high schools.

Today Title VI supports primarily the area study centers at a variety of universities across the nation. The federal funds provide only one out of eight dollars needed to run the programs. Many of the centers are on shaky ground, not knowing from year to year whether they will survive. In 1970, there were 106 such centers, but by 1980, only 80 survive, some of them barely breathing. Federal funding for these centers, which specialize in Asian studies, Latin American studies, or another geographic area, has risen from $15,800,000 in 1967 to $17 million (part of which is shared with other programs) in 1979. However, because of inflation, there has been a fairly sharp actual drop in federal support of these vital programs.

One of the better known programs is the Mutual Education and Cultural Exchange Act of 1961, also known as the Fulbright-Hays Act. This act provides for "promoting modern foreign language training and area studies in the United States schools" by encouraging U.S. teachers to visit other countries, and for the teachers of other nations to visit the United States. More than 150,000 scholars, teachers, and students have traveled from one country to another to study under the Fulbright-Hays program. The funding for these programs, when inflation is considered, has gradually declined. In real, noninflated dollars, for example, this portion of the Fulbright-Hays program of fellowships declined more than 25 percent between fiscal years 1970 and 1977. In 1967, the teacher exchange portion of the Fulbright-Hays program received an appropriation of approximately $3 million and, in 1979, the same amount—again, a significant drop in actual purchasing power, particularly when the drop in the dollar on international exchanges is considered.

These programs have resulted in a tremendous reservoir of goodwill for the United States among people in sensitive leadership positions in almost every country. Incomprehensibly, in 1974, the Nixon Administration recommended no funding at all for the Fulbright-Hays programs. Fortunately, Congress did not accept that suggestion. Nevertheless, Congress has sensed no great need to provide more adequate funding of international studies and foreign language programs. In fact, in a budget of more than half a trillion dollars, not much attention is paid to such studies. Indifference, rather than hostility, characterizes the congressional attitude. There has been enough support to keep most programs operating at a minimal level, but no more. Dr. Hayden's study shows that in 1967, twenty-six departments and agencies received a total of $40.6 million for international affairs research study projects of one variety or another. But by 1977, only twenty departments received funds, and the total had dropped to $32.6 million. In constant dollars that is a drop of 52 percent.

The year 1967 was the high point in appropriation dollars. This followed a Special Message to Congress by President Lyndon B. Johnson, on February 2, 1966, "proposing international education and health programs." He outlined a specific legislative agenda, most of which did not emerge; it centered on four aims: " . . . to strengthen our capacity for international educational cooperation; to stimulate exchange with students and teachers of other lands; to assist the progress of education in developing nations; [and] to build bridges of international understanding." Much of what President Johnson proposed did not receive funding, but he gave the cause a new thrust. After the 1967 peak, funding has diminished.

The loss in appropriation dollars easily hides a deeper, unpleasant reality. Many believe that most federal dollars are wasted anyway, and that if a program is cut somewhat, no great harm is done other than the loss of a few unnecessary chieftains in Washington. The losses here, on the contrary, have been concrete and measurable.

The following table shows the number of foreign language and area studies fellowships, in a sampling of key languages, that were awarded in 1973 and in 1977.

Language	No. of Fellowships Awarded	
	1973	1977
Swahili	44	12
Chinese	181	105
Japanese	121	83
Arabic	136	108
Russian	118	61

The trend is unfortunately clear. These losses cannot be explained in terms of a rational legislative and administrative response to a pressing national need. Rather, the foreign language program that has emerged is largely unplanned and meets only a small portion of the national need.

Constructing policy is a little like building a house. If you plan carefully for it, there still will be problems. But if you build without planning, the problems are much greater. In foreign language policy, we have built without a plan, without asking what we are building or what we should build.

In 1978, a group of academic leaders looked at the history and status of foreign language teaching and concluded: "Language education in the United States would appear to be at a turning point . . . existing problems cannot be solved without a measure of centralization. . . ." [3] A growing number of signals sends the same message, that we have reached a point where this national concern must be expressed in some explicit way. In May 1976, Representative Albert Quie, a Republican member of Congress who would be elected Governor of Minnesota in 1978, told his House colleagues on the floor:

> If we pull back on this and say, let us leave it to the states or local communities, they have no more reason to put up money to understand other parts of the world than they have to put up a portion of our defense system. It is important nationally for our people to understand other parts of the world. . . . It is a national responsibility.

· 2 ·

The Trade Gap

The chances that a lawyer, a banker, an engineer, a chemist, will be sent at some time or other in his career to a Common Market country, to the Middle East, to Africa or South America, are ten times greater in 1975 than they were twenty-five years ago. . . . Unless they show some facility in a foreign language and some interest in the people whose culture, tastes, and frame of mind differ profoundly from their own, they will be losers. . . .

Henri Peyre [1]

I finally decided to concentrate on learning Spanish around 1965, and after I became proficient in 1967, my business with Spanish-speaking countries increased from nothing to over twenty million dollars yearly.

André Crispin [2]

Mississippi's outlook is being hampered by her traditionally conservative distrust of foreigners and all things foreign. Under the category of "foreign," alongside the slowly growing population of Hispanics, Orientals, and Africans, one must also place foreign languages and foreign cultures.

Barbara C. Dease [3]

We are in a new economic era, measured by quality.

Not many years ago, the stamp *Made in Japan* meant to the American mind an inferior product. Every American old enough to recall those days knows that this has changed. A consumer survey in Germany found fewer than 40 percent "confident" about the reliability of U.S.-made electrical products, while 91 percent had confidence in German products.[4]

And we are in a new era, measured by quantity.

After World War II, the United States possessed the world's only nuclear weapons and, along with Canada and Australia, were the only participants in that conflict that had a virtually undamaged economy. We were the world's economic superpower. No other nation came close to our technical know-how, our productive and transporting capacities. We sold our products readily throughout the world.

Immediately after World War II, exports were distorted in our favor. The lead continued; in every year from 1954 to 1971, the United States exported more than it imported. In 1971, however, we had a trade deficit of $2.7 billion. Since that time we have had only two years with trade surpluses. The 1978 trade deficit was a tenfold increase over 1971, up to $28.5 billion. For the Japanese fiscal year ending March 31, 1978, Japan had a surplus in trade with the United States of $10 billion. In two years, the value of the dollar, compared to the yen, dropped 37 percent. When the dollar dropped in value, the OPEC nations naturally raised the price of oil, creating even larger U.S. trade deficits.

CB radios are a concrete example of the new economic era. At first, we manufactured all of them. But visitors from Japan—which had no CB radios—took the time to study our language and our culture; they saw how widely the radios were used here. Soon the Japanese had perfected their own product; today, 95 percent of new CB radios sold in the United States are manufactured in Japan.

By 1979, Switzerland's per capita gross national product exceeded the United States's GNP by 45 percent; Denmark, Sweden, and West Germany were ahead of us. Japan was only 7 percent behind us. All four of these countries surpass our skill in languages, one factor responsible for the shift in economic pattern.

An obvious way to respond to this shift—and a politically popular way—is to set up additional trade barriers through higher tariffs, more restrictive quotas, and a mass of administrative red tape to slow down the inward flow of foreign commerce. That spirit of protectionism is alive and well in the Congress. But protectionism is a simplistic answer, which, like most simplistic answers, is wrong. It invites economic disaster.

Protectionism will increase the rate of inflation because, on the average, imported goods will cost more. Trade restrictions ultimately deprive U.S. workers of jobs. It's an illusion to imagine that duties can be boosted unilaterally. Other nations will simply reciprocate.

Imports frequently have an adverse impact on a specific industry in the United States, in one congressional district, or in one particular state. And when employees and employers ask for protection from outside competition, there are seldom any balancing calls from the more dispersed consumer population that would benefit from lower-priced imports. To add just a little more import tax seems a simple and innocuous step in the present illogical and inconsistent pattern of duties. Our customs duties vary from 55 percent on some kinds of china to 3 percent on automobiles, from 22.5 percent on cigarette lighters to 4 percent on small diamonds, from 17.5 percent on toys to 2.5 percent on cultured pearls, from 8.5 percent on wooden chairs to 5 percent on all other wooden furniture.

Such duties are an easy target for a business or a union or a member of Congress. Why should the duty on wooden furniture be 70 percent less than the duty on wooden chairs? The manufacturers of all types of wooden furniture other than chairs are probably now importuning their senators and representatives and the International Trade Commission to raise the duty from 5 percent to 8.5 percent. More than a century and a half ago, Macaulay wrote: "Free trade, one of the greatest blessings which a government can confer on a people, is in almost every country unpopular." [5]

Workers and businesses do deserve some protection. The trade-related unemployment compensation provisions for employees and the loan provisions to help corporations adjust to some new line of operation are now inadequate. Still the long-range answer must be to raise export consciousness and capacity. The United States sales abroad are well over $100 billion annually; in 1978 they were $144 billion. One of every eight American manufacturing jobs is dependent on exports, and one of every three American agricultural acres is used to grow produce for export. Future policies must strengthen, not jeopardize, this important segment of our economy.

Few statistics more graphically illustrate the problem than this table of exports and imports of major Northeastern U.S. ports in 1975:

Ports	1975 Cargo Imports (in 1000s of short tons)	1975 Cargo Exports (in 1000s of short tons)
New York City	48,966	6,726
Boston, MA	5,988	547
Paulsboro, NJ	11,811	118
New Haven, CT	1,765	162
Portland, ME	23,159	16
Fall River, MA	1,571	——— *
Salem, MA	1,324	——— *
Portsmouth, NH	1,371	13
Camden-Gloucester, NJ	1,263	375

Albany, NY	1,734	534
Marcus Hook, PA	12,322	160
Penn Manor, PA	6,930	22
Philadelphia, PA	28,386	5,104
Providence, RI	1,135	295

* Fewer than 500 tons.

While cargo tonnage and value of the product do not precisely equate, one obvious defect of the Northeast United States is a failure to produce adequately for export. And while these statistics are more dramatic than for most areas, the imbalance is national. An adverse balance of trade contributes to the decline of the dollar and adds to our inflation. Of the 9.2 percent inflation in the United States in 1978, between one-tenth and one-fifth could be attributed to the drop in the value of the dollar.

Of the top exporting nations in 1978, the United States is still ahead in export dollars, but is barely ahead of West Germany, a nation smaller than the state of Oregon.

Country	1978 Exports (*in billions*) *of U.S. dollars*)
United States	143.7
West Germany	142.3
Japan	98.4
France	79.4
United Kingdom	71.7
Italy	56.1
Netherlands	50.1
Canada	47.9
Belgium	45.0
Saudi Arabia	37.8
Sweden	23.8
Switzerland	23.6

Iran	22.5
Australia	14.4
Spain	13.1
South Africa	12.8
Taiwan	12.7
Korea	12.5
Austria	12.2
Denmark	11.9

Nor is the per capita breakdown favorable to the United States; it is sixteenth in rank.

Country	Per Capita 1978 Exports (*in U.S. dollars*)
Saudi Arabia	$4,736.84
Belgium	4,573.17
Switzerland	3,751.99
Netherlands	3,583.69
Sweden	2,870.93
Denmark	2,328.77
West Germany	2,322.89
Canada	2,020.24
Austria	1,624.50
France	1,483.00
Australia	1,425.00
United Kingdom	1,283.80
Italy	986.46
Japan	852.02
Taiwan	741.82
United States	655.19
Iran	628.32
South Africa	461.26
Spain	346.84
Korea	318.80

Short-term Band-Aid solutions for the trade gap problem abound—most of them flawed. However, there are some essential long-range answers:

1. Greater expenditures on research. Tax law revision and other steps can encourage basic research. (If we can improve relations with the other major military superpower, the Soviet Union, fewer of our research dollars will be consumed by military weaponry.)

2. Improved productivity. The more we can produce per man-hour and per dollar invested, the more we will sell abroad because of lower per unit costs.

3. Greater business sensitivity to, and aggressiveness in, the international market. Of 300,000 U.S. manufacturers or producers, fewer than 10 percent export. Many of those who could profit most from the export market ignore that market. Estimates run as high as 80 percent on the percentage of business transactions that will become international in the 1980–90 decade.

4. More aggressive promotion of export trade by federal and state governments. We are one of the few major industrial nations without a department of international trade. There is also some evidence that our system of commercial attachés assigned to embassies abroad is much less effective in promoting U.S. business opportunities than it might be.

5. A quantum leap in the study of foreign languages, and with it, a sensitivity to other cultures. The most intensive study of inflation ever undertaken by a congressional committee, the Task Force on Inflation of the House Budget Committee, in 1979, recommended expansion of exports, and stimulation of language study. "We are not adequately studying languages and cultures of other countries," it said. "And as a result we are not getting to know our customers. Not surprisingly, we do not sell as well as we should." [6]

A Chicago area businessman, Joel Honigberg, president of the Overseas Sales and Marketing Association, speaks five languages. He has toured Chicago area high schools giving lectures to foreign language students, urging them to combine language skills and business training: "There are only about 1,000 college students who graduate each year with majors in international trade—a field which we call geotrade. There are jobs for at least 200,000 geotrade experts." [7]

Visiting in Paris, Jack Kolbert, president of Monterey Institute of International Studies, asked a Japanese businessman, there to negotiate a big contract, what language he thought was most important for world trade. In fluent French, the Japanese businessman replied, "Sir, the most useful international language in world trade is not necessarily English, but rather it is the language of your client." [8]

The largest Scandinavian corporation is not as familiar as names like Volvo, SKF, SAS, Saab; it is Dèt Ostasiatiske Kompagni, the East Asian Company Ltd. (EAC). It traded with mainland China long before the United States did. *Newsweek* reported that EAC employees have studied profiles of leading Chinese trade officials. "And almost all of the company's top officers speak Chinese." [9] EAC has a "basic training period" for their new employees. One of their personnel officers says of this program:

> During the basic training period here at Head Office [Copenhagen] the young trainees receive the following language training:
>
> | | | |
> |---|---|---|
> | 1st year: | English | 3 hours per week and |
> | | German | 3 hours per week |
> | 2nd year: | English | 4 hours per week |
> | 3rd year: | French | 3 hours per week or |
> | | Spanish | 4 hours per week or |
> | | Portuguese | 4 hours per week |
>
> When they start this training they normally have had 6 to 8 years' studies in English, 5 to 6 years in German, and 2 to 4 years in French. . . .
>
> This is the basic training, but when the young people arrive

overseas they immediately have to learn the language and try to understand the culture of the country to which they have been posted and, as an example, we can mention that during the first three to six months after their arrival in Japan they are not working in our organization there, but using all their time for an intensified course in the Japanese language, culture, and history.

A reasonable command of the local language and understanding of the background of the country in which our people work open many doors. Besides we consider it only common courtesy towards the country in which our people are guests that they acquire such knowledge.[10]

Paul Hirsch, retired American business executive with years of overseas experience, confirms that

very often foreign language knowledge makes the difference between success and failure. Dealing with the prospective foreign buyer of American goods in his local tongue can produce unexpected results, especially in pursuing new methods of trade, necessitated by many foreign countries' shortage of hard currency. The answer in such cases is "barter and/or switch" transactions (countertrade) to be executed without cash flow. However, these rather complicated case-by-case deals can best be initiated and carried out on the spot and by negotiating in local languages.[11]

A *Business Week* article noted that one of the keys to success for an overseas American business leader is that the executive and the executive's family must have a "desire to learn a new culture and, in many instances, a new language." [12]

Frank A. Weil, former Assistant Secretary of Commerce for Industry and Trade, puts it well:

Our linguistic parochialism has had a negative effect on our trade balance. In fact, it is one of the most subtle nontariff barriers to our export expansion. . . . America does not export enough, 6–8 percent of our GNP as opposed to 15–25 percent of the GNPs of Germany and Japan. . . . Part of the reason the Japanese and the Germans sell so effectively is that they have gone to the trouble of learning about us and adapting the products they export to our tastes and markets. An impressive number of their businessmen have learned our language, and foreign business students usually have international studies as part of the curriculum. . . .

The government can do many things to improve the export capacity of the American economy. It can do away with unnecessary impediments to exports and replace them with incentives. But only the business community can make the sales. Language promotion, like export promotion, would benefit the American business community and, in turn, our economy.[13]

Because it is only ninety miles from Cuba, Miami has developed an effective capacity for bilingualism. Manufacturers and sales representatives throughout Latin America have found they can now do business in Miami in their own language—thanks, in large part, to the influx of Cuban refugees. Exports from Miami have more than doubled since 1970, and Miami has become the new center of tourism for Latin American tourists, who spend well over $300 million in that city annually.

In 1974–75, Olympus Research Corporation sent questionnaires on foreign language needs to 5,640 U.S.-based companies; 1,261 who responded reported that they have 60,678 positions in which foreign language competence is necessary or preferable. The survey brought this response from an Ohio executive:

There is a rapidly increasing need for foreign language skills in our organization and every organization. However, we find there is great difficulty in hiring people in the Midwest, where little contact with foreigners or foreign-speaking people is obtainable. The schools . . . are not set up properly to teach language skills. Therefore, in general, we hire third-country nationals in the country where we are in operation. . . . All of our top management positions outside the United States—such as technical directors, regional managers, sales personnel, and managing directors—are held by foreigners. Most of our American technicians, we find, are not capable of adding language skills at the present time, so we have to send them out and then use local interpreters. There is definite need in the United States ... to develop more and more interest in language schools and training as our business becomes more and more international.[14]

Another survey of the nation's top corporations doing business overseas found staffing practices "infrequently systematic, too frequently haphazard, and occasionally chaotic." Among their findings:

Executives who do not speak the host language in a non-English speaking nation can have great difficulty managing subordinates because of the inability to communicate verbally.... The Overseas managers questioned in this study place significantly more weight on the language-training factor than do the foreign operations managers directing and coordinating from the United States.[15]

A 1973 survey of those who had been students in area study centers at universities and are now applying that knowledge in academia, government, or business, found continuing

debates about whether one needs a command of a local language in order to do significant work on a given world area, particularly in those countries where colonial regimes have left a substantial elite capable of using a European language and where a large proportion of the scholarly and official publication discourse is in a European language. It seems that one hears less and less of this argument as the time since the departure of the colonial regimes increases and as the level of analysis drop from ... the foreign-educated minority to non-elite and native groups.[16]

The survey asked how important knowledge of a language is, and 58.7 percent responding said it is "impossible to work without it"; 30.1 percent described it as "important, but can do work without it"; 7.9 percent, "helpful, but not important"; and only 3.3 percent, "do not need it."

A successful Mobil Oil Corp. intern program takes students overseas for a year to learn language, culture, and the overseas business operation. Other corporations are now following their example.

The international market is in some respects similar to the domestic market. For several years I was in the newspaper and job printing business, publishing weekly newspapers in small communities and printing everything from business forms to funeral notices. I bought newsprint from Pioneer Paper Company because they had the best price, and envelopes from the Roodhouse Envelope Company for the same reason. But for most supplies, competitive prices were fairly close, and then I bought the salesperson rather than the product. The salesperson who knew about my family and my interests, who had read an article I had written—who "spoke my language"—got me as a customer. If someone had come to my office speaking only Japanese, he might have had the best product in the world but I would probably not have bought from him. The world market is no different. To sell effectively in Italy, speak Italian.

A survey of Illinois exporting firms found that they used Spanish, German, Polish, Japanese, Russian, Portuguese, Italian, French, Greek, Korean, Tagalog, Arabic, Rumanian, Dutch, Chinese, Hungarian, Serbian, Urdu, Indonesian, Danish, and Farsi. A Kansas survey added Guarani, Norwegian, Finnish, and Swedish.

I do not want to oversimplify the case, for language ability alone does not make a good salesperson. A good product to sell, an ability to get along with people, and a willingness to work hard are also requisites. But trust is essential to a good business relationship, and it is difficult to achieve trust through a translator. The potential customer senses cultural arrogance.

In this nation's most widely circulated magazine, the *Reader's Digest,* an article about Japan-U.S. trade relations said, "Many U.S. businesses with export potential seem to lack drive or know-how." It told of an American businessman who tried to press doormats upon a Japanese, "apparently not knowing that Japanese remove their shoes before entering a home—and thus don't need doormats." [17]

Body by Fisher, describing a General Motors product, came out "Corpse by Fisher" in Flemish, and that did not help sales. Schweppes Tonic was advertised in Italy as "bathroom water." Cue toothpaste, a Colgate-Palmolive product, was advertised in France with no translation errors, but *Cue* happens to be the name of a widely circulated pornographic book there about oral sex, and the ads produced laughs rather than sales. A laundry soap ad in Quebec promised users "clean genitals." *Come Alive With Pepsi* almost appeared in the Chinese version of the *Reader's Digest* as "Pepsi brings your ancestors back from the grave." In the German edition of the magazine, the ad said, "Come alive out of the grave." A major ad campaign in green did not sell in Malaysia, where green symbolizes death and disease.[18] An airline operating out of Brazil advertised that it had plush "rendezvous lounges" on its jets, unaware that in Portuguese, *rendezvous* implied a room for making love.[19]

We must learn the language and culture of others if we expect to sell.

A Kansas company, discovering a substantial potential foreign market for its product, decided to work through a foreign intermediary and found that unsatisfactory. It then tried a widely known U.S. translation and foreign assistance firm, but it was too slow and cumbersome. The U.S. company finally gave up exporting altogether. The lack of language skills had ruined a good business opportunity.[20]

Edwin O. Reischauer describes the situation he found as

U.S. Ambassador in Japan: "The armed services took pains to prepare their men for their tasks much better than did the economic branches of our government." Most military and naval officers attached to the embassy had received a year of Japanese language study, followed by a year of Pentagon service connected with Japan, before they were sent to Tokyo. "The economic and commercial officers, by contrast, were lucky if they had had any previous contact with Japanese affairs. I am not suggesting that our military expertise on other countries is greater than it need be, but rather that our non-military expertise is seriously deficient." [21]

"Trade is a social act," John Stuart Mill wrote in 1859 in his essay, *On Liberty*. It is just as true today. And social acts require language communication skills.

The needs of business are not limited to salesmanship skills. United States business leaders who expect significant growth must show a sensitivity to the culture of other countries, adapt their products, accommodate to other patterns of life.

Some countries are eager to have certain U.S. imports. Kazuo Aichi, a member of the Japanese Diet (House of Representatives), discussed the trade deficit problem candidly. He sent a letter urging me to "call upon your business circles . . . for their positive approach to our market." He enclosed a booklet put together by Japanese economic interests explaining (in English) to foreign businesses how to get a bigger share of the Japanese market.[22] It urges them to study "the needs of Japanese customers." It advised prospective sellers from abroad "to visit some Japanese department stores and supermarkets and observe on the spot what kinds of products are sold and at what price." The booklet concludes: "The decisive factor is the degree of enthusiasm in exporting countries to expand sales to Japan. We believe that the Japanese market has great promise. But to exploit the opportunities in Japan, foreign businesses must first find out what the

Japanese consumers want, [and] tailor products to fit that Japanese market."

International business relationships extend beyond importing and exporting. Sizable portions of U.S. business operations are actually overseas, including: construction machinery, 27 percent overseas; farm machinery, 27 percent overseas; drug industry, 31 percent overseas; tires, 22 percent; office machinery, 20 percent; soaps and detergents, 20 percent; motor vehicles, 18 percent; soft drinks, 18 percent. Many of the largest American corporations—including Ford and Caterpillar—now earn more than 50 percent of their annual profits from overseas sales and operations.

At the same time, foreign investment in the United States has been growing. By 1979, foreign investments in the United States had reached $245 billion in firms employing well over one million U.S. citizens. Even that neighborhood supermarket, A & P, now has German ownership. U.S. investments abroad are about $300 billion.

E. A. Costanzo, vice-president of Citibank in New York, told a New York University symposium, "The young man [or woman] who graduates from one of our business schools without the realization of the scope and thrust of multinational business is as unprepared for the reality of our economy as the young man [or woman] who graduates without a little accounting knowledge." [23]

Multinational businesses are a reality, and like most realities, have their pluses and their minuses. People who yearn for the corner grocery store to replace the supermarket are dreaming of a day that will never return, and those who hope for the disappearance and demise of the multinational corporation are building hopes on a foundation of straw. Since the multinational corporation is here to stay, it should be shaped so that it benefits the economy of our own nation and humanity as a whole.

Research is essential to economic progress in a business

and a nation. Historian and language scene observer S. Frederick Starr made an important observation:

> However large the role of English is at present, its relative importance is bound to decline in the future as modernization goes forward in more parts of the globe. Every year the number of journals and books published in languages other than English increases. As more nations involve themselves in the production of new knowledge, the number of first-class research reports appearing in Japanese, Russian, Portuguese, or Chinese will grow apace.[24]

A letter from the president of the American Translators Association to President Carter expressed a sense of desperation:

> The latest developments in science and technology are now being published in more than 70 languages of some 100 countries. Even though English still accounts for about 45% of this material, and another 35% is published in Russian, German, and French, some 20% appears in the less well known languages. The information value of Japanese publications has increased remarkably over the past few years, while Hungarian has become very important for electronics, Swedish for metallurgy, power engineering, shipbuilding, and communications systems, and Finnish for woodworking, pulp and paper technology, icebreaker construction, etc. Polish, Czech, Bulgarian, and Rumanian technical literature is also becoming important, as is Spanish and Portuguese. When an agreement is finally reached that will permit us access to the technical literature of the People's Republic of China we shall have several decades of development to study, and there is less than a handful of people in the United States today who are competent to translate technical Chinese.[25]

This letter to President Carter cites a five-page litany of losses to this nation, both in the public and private sector.

When U.S. business or professional people go to an international meeting in Germany, for example, they assume that

that meeting will be conducted in English. But gradually such assumptions are changing. People abroad resent the cultural arrogance that takes it for granted that when U.S. businesses hold a meeting "in *our* country" it will be "in *our* language" and when they hold it "in *your* country it will be in *our* language." Business and professional people who want to keep up on the latest research and developments will in the future be compelled to speak and to understand other languages.

Dr. Carl Zimmer, managing director of the West German firm of Interfinanz, which specializes in mergers and acquisitions, created a minor stir with a blunt article in the *Christian Science Monitor,* headlined, "Nobody Likes to Work for the Americans." Zimmer worte:

> There are language problems; many American managers, who have been stationed abroad with a subsidiary of a U.S. corporation, fail to speak the host country's language even after living in the country for many years. When a major American bank acquired majority interest in a European bank, the manager sent there by the U.S. bank demanded that his colleagues and employees conduct all business in English. . . . U.S. corporations that are profitable and are well respected by the public have hired host-country managers to run their operations, or they employ Americans who make an effort to become familiar with their new environment.[26]

One of the most impressive documents on U.S. business, its relationship to other countries, and its relationship to U.S. education, is *Business and International Education,*[27] funded by the Exxon Education Foundation, and prepared by two task forces of business and education leaders, working under the auspices of the American Council on Education. The business representation on these task forces included officials from firms as varied as General Electric, IBM, First National City Bank, Arthur Anderson and Company, B.F. Goodrich, Sunkist Growers, Carnation, and ALCOA. Among their findings:

• In the future, most businessmen will "need an ability to understand and anticipate ... economic and political developments on the international scene."

• High percentages of individuals becoming presidents of corporations have had no international work experience, many managers with international responsibilities have had "no international studies ... to prepare them for such international responsibilities."

• More than 75 percent of those receiving doctorates in the field of business have had *no* international business courses during their graduate studies. (Another source refers to graduates of business schools as "linguistically paralyzed.")

• One survey of large firms doing business abroad found that a knowledge of another language is considered the most important type of capability for an overseas assignment. Language training is the most important part of predeparture training for managers going overseas. An Exxon executive commented on a list of possible criteria for selection of an overseas manager: "Apart from the right wife and an ability to speak or learn foreign languages, all proposed criteria are unacceptable."

• While the need for competence in foreign languages has been increasing, the number of college students studying languages has been decreasing.

• "The drop of interest in and study of foreign languages is both a symptom of the increasing provincialism and a cause of future provincialism in the thinking, and voting, of the U.S. populace. ... It is clearly in the interest of business that this trend be reversed. It is also clearly in the interest of government that this trend be reversed."

• Eighty-five percent of the businesses surveyed believe there will be a growing need for people in business with a working knowledge of a foreign language.

• People enter the field of business from all types of academic backgrounds, not just business (a minority have been trained in business), but fewer than 10 percent of university students now study a modern foreign language, less than one-half of 1 percent now study abroad, and a very high percentage now graduate without ever having had a course about the history, politics, economics, or culture of a foreign country or area.

The task force follows that dismal piece of news with this comment:

> The Task Force ... feels that a true university education should be understood to include the international dimension. For education, in its essence and by definition, should result in the elimination of provincialism. Without this, the graduate is destined to be an uninformed citizen of the most powerful country in the world, and will be inadequately prepared to be a future manager in a high percentage of U.S. business firms.

The group called upon the American Council on Education to help reverse the present trends, to "encourage universities to examine existing foreign language requirements, to improve language sequences for non-majors," and to encourage or even require all students to study a foreign language.

Another survey found that 14 percent of the businesses responding have business dealings with non-English-speaking business people overseas and another 15 percent expect to have such dealings in the next five years.[28] This survey also noted a trend toward expanding business abroad, "even by firms of moderate size." But significantly, 46 percent have no employees with foreign language skills.

While the effort to improve trade is centered at the federal level, the action to improve language programs primarily must come from state government and local school boards. In a healthy development, state and local governments—along with Chambers of Commerce—have begun to move more aggressively to pursue international trade.

However, when North Carolina, Georgia, and Illinois, for

example, send trade delegations abroad, there is often a tendency for the press to treat such endeavors as "junkets." Some persons may indeed go simply for the pleasure of the trip—just as some do on congressional trips. Nevertheless, these overseas visits have resulted in substantial economic benefit to their states. Combining a forward thrust in foreign language programs in the schools with trade delegations abroad can be a winning combination, as North Carolina has discovered. North Carolina now has more than 150 foreign firms in its state with an investment of well over $1 billion. Illinois businesses have found international trade fairs helpful in overcoming "barriers of foreign languages, unfamiliar markets and credit systems." One report says that participating Illinois businessmen have received approximately $250,000 in business for each $1,000 they have invested.[29]

Houston business leaders also understand their economic ties to the rest of the world. The Houston Chamber of Commerce reports that "international interests now concentrating in Houston will, in the future, require personnel with specialized job-related training in world trade. Also, Third World nations which do not fit the pattern of older countries will require country-by-country training on specific conditions in each such country." The Houston Chamber of Commerce appointed a task force to review the capacity of schools of higher education in the Houston area to meet the area's anticipated needs in international trade.[30]

"Let us not wait for the campus to come to us. It is in our interest to seek out the campus," their report states; and they did precisely that. It also notes the international business courses available, and reports that you can take Swahili at the University of Houston (as one example).

It describes the 2,400 foreign students in the Houston area from ninety different countries as "a potential international resource." It recommends that for business people who expect to go abroad, an "expedited instruction" program be developed to provide quickly "a working knowledge of language, history, customs, commerce and essential specifics."

The weakness of the otherwise solid Houston Chamber of Commerce report, and a serious one, is that it wholly ignores the elementary and secondary schools. Every ·Chamber of Commerce in the nation might well produce a similar review—and it takes no federal funding or federal initiative.

The trade gap will be a permanent, debilitating economic wound unless long-range steps are promptly taken to close that gap. One of those steps is to start speaking with the rest of the world, developing a generation of business leaders who understand that it is essential to have knowledge of another culture and of another language and who follow through by acquiring that knowledge or by securing key personnel with that knowledge.

· 3 ·

The Security Problem

Most area specialist officers in the Executive Branch
[of the federal government], including the intelligence
services, do not, and usually cannot, read the materials
of greatest concern to them in the original, and cannot
converse with their foreign counterparts beyond
pleasantries in the other language.

John Wilson Lewis [1]

I had . . . to wrestle with the problem of the fundamental nature of international security during my tenure
as U.S. Secretary of Defense. . . . We still tend to con-
ceive of national security . . . almost solely as a state of
armed readiness: a vast, awesome arsenal of weaponry.
But . . . as one reflects on the problem more deeply it is
clear that force alone does not guarantee security, and
that a nation can reach a point at which it does not buy
more security for itself simply by buying more military
hardware.

Robert McNamara [2]

What we do not know can harm us.

Stephen K. Bailey [3]

Sometimes our failure to understand languages is a security
threat in the most immediate sense. The kidnappers of U.S.
Ambassador to Afghanistan Adolph Dubs took him to the
Kabul Hotel. Before the tragic slaying, so the *Washington
Star* reports: "[U.S.] Embassy officials had a brief chance to
seize the initiative because they reached the hotel before

Afghan police. But no one in the American party spoke fluent Dari or Pushtu, the two most widely used Afghan languages, or fluent Russian."[4] Language is essential to security and safety in this multilingual world.

Some years ago in India, I spoke with the acting chief of the U.S. Embassy. I asked him how many people on the embassy staff spoke Hindi. "I don't believe any do," he replied, "but we can speak to educated people here in English." Had I asked the same question of the Soviet ambassador I would not have received the same reply.

The ultimate aim of security is to keep this nation safe from a foreign attack. It is impossible to keep our country secure and to protect our citizens abroad unless the world's oppressed have some sense of hope, unless the world's merchants are able to trade without fear of violence, and unless the world's armies are free of constant apprehension and are not too taut. To move in that direction—literally, the direction of survival—it is imperative that U.S. policy be geared toward (1) understanding potential foes; (2) reinforcing ties of friendship with allies and with potential adversaries; and (3) communicating directly with the millions of the world's most desperate peoples.

Yet it is easier to generate congressional support for a new weapons system costing billions that will ultimately make us less secure than for less tangible, but more constructive projects costing 1 percent of that amount. "Friendship," "understanding," "communication" seem to have less appeal to national pride and bravado than a weapons system has; nor do they have as many lobbyists.

Officials of the Defense Language Institute's Foreign Language Center, an arm of the Department of Defense, consider languages necessary to our security. They are distressed at the state of affairs in our language capacity. Here is part of their litany of complaints:

Foreign language enrollment in both schools and colleges has progressively declined during the past decade. This decline has meant that fewer and fewer military personnel taking language courses in the Defense Foreign Language Program have had any previous foreign language education.

Every year the total number of persons who can communicate in foreign languages decreases, while every year the nation's need for linguists in defense, in foreign affairs, and in the private sector increases. . . .

Many countries train their foreign language military students twice as long as the United States and utilize them for longer periods of specialized duty. . . .

Translation-interpretation services and dictionary-glossary development are not only completely decentralized but are also . . . inadequate to meet Government needs. For example, a German military dictionary-glossary developed in World War II has not been updated. . . .

The category of the less commonly taught languages account for only one percent of the nation's secondary school foreign language enrollments. Yet these are the languages spoken by over 80% of the world's population, and several of them have for many years been classified as "strategic" or "critical" from the point of view of the national interest of the United States. . . .

For more than 30 years Americans have been stationed abroad with little formal language training or cultural orientation required or available even when occupying positions in which language proficiency was an absolute requirement for accomplishment of assigned missions.[5]

A 1979 study by James Ruchti showed forty-three positions in the State Department requiring professional proficiency in Russian and thirty-five Foreign Service officers with that proficiency; a total of 4,943 positions in the federal government require Russian proficiency, but there are only 3,206 persons who can fill that need; of the 4,576 positions in "defense-security" requiring knowledge of Russian, 3,039 persons in these jobs know the language. The Russian language capabilities of our federal government are limited—

and our knowledge of the languages in some of the non-Russian republics of the Soviet Union is almost nonexistent. We do not have the language capacity to match our incredible technical knowledge of the Soviet Union, knowledge gained, in large measure, by satellite pictures of movements of men and military equipment; and infrared satellite exposure that reveals locations of missile installations by plotting areas in the earth from which heat is escaping. We have no comparable wealth of understanding between the leaders and peoples of the United States and the Soviet Union, ultimately more important to the security of both nations than the mountains of data and pictures we collect on each other.

When Hugh A. Mulligan of the Associated Press was in Vietnam, he received a request from his London news editor to write a story about "laundry forms." It turned out later that the assignment was for a story on land reforms.[6] Language had been garbled in the transmission even between two English-speaking people, a trivial error. A misunderstanding or misinterpretation between a Soviet leader and an American leader, on the other hand, could bring on disaster.

While U.S. and Soviet expenditures for armaments increase, the number of students of the Russian language in the United States declines—which seems absolutely irrational whether from the viewpoint of the hard-liners who expect to fight or from the viewpoint of those of us who hope to avoid such a disaster. There are more teachers of English in the Soviet Union than there are students of Russian in the entire United States. There are more Soviet citizens studying English in Leningrad than there are students of the Russian language in the United States. But this is only part of the story. During the academic years 1975–76 to 1978–79, 52 colleges and universities in the United States dropped the teaching of Russian. I visited the University of North Carolina at Charlotte recently, with its above-average language program—fewer than fifteen students were enrolled in Russian.

Uncertainty of financial status has weakened many Soviet research centers at our universities. Some have closed, some have declined. The Russian Research Center at Harvard slipped from an annual budget of $300,000 in the late 1950s to about $50,000 in 1976–77. A more hopeful sign has been the creation of the Kennan Institute of Soviet Studies at the Smithsonian Institution in Washington, D.C., and of IREX (International Research and Exchange Programs), an academic consortium, which promotes and coordinates exchange programs with Eastern European countries. But still, we spend more to construct three-fourths of a mile of interstate highway than on exchange programs with the Eastern European countries, including the Soviet Union, when the space program exchanges are excluded. The Soviets and the Warsaw Pact nations would like to exchange more students and teachers than our schools can afford. Of the thousands of Soviets denied a chance to visit and study here, many will undoubtedly advance into positions of leadership. Many will move into positions of influence in their local communities. Fortunately, enough ice had melted—prior to the Afghanistan invasion—so that in the last ten years 600 exchanges have occurred covering a full academic year, and thousands of exchanges of shorter duration. It is not enough. Exchanges in sociology, economics, and other policy fields (as distinct from the hard sciences) are down; we have reduced and/or eliminated funds for exchanges in these fields. Exchange programs seem to have low priority.

In the entire Southeastern United States, only one school, Florida State University, offers a master's degree in Russian. Nationally, Russian language courses are fewer and poorly attended, and Soviet study programs are suffering. As one foreign language bulletin noted:

Russian studies in the United States, in which impressive strengths in scholarship have been developed in the period since World War II, are now in trouble. . . . There is scarcely any level of activity in Russian studies, from initial language training to the most sophisticated research, that is today not faced with, or threatened by, a decline in scope and vigor. The implications of this trend, from the standpoint of the country at large, are serious.[7]

And the situation has not improved since that article appeared.

"Soviet Talks Shook Visiting Senators" read the headline of a December 24, 1978 *Washington Post* article by Robert G. Kaiser. The Soviets came across as "arrogant and abrasive" to many of the Senators, especially those who had not visited the Soviet Union before. Senator John Durkin of New Hampshire was quoted as saying that it would take Americans another generation to understand the Soviet Union, and the Soviets two generations to understand us. When the talks (which tended to be Soviet lectures rather than discussions) shifted to dinner at the homes of Soviet officials, Senator Henry Bellmon of Oklahoma (one of the Senate's finest members, unfortunately retiring in 1980) proposed a toast "to the past, when we were allies, and to the future, when we can be friends in the daytime as well as at night." More such pleasant visits in homes, more genuine discussions would advance peace more than sermons preached by both sides. But for these visits and discussions to take place, people must be able to talk with one another, and that requires knowledge of a language.

In May and June of 1978, I served as one of the United States delegates to the United Nations Session on Disarmament. During the first days of the session, Foreign Minister Andrei Gromyko invited the United States delegation to meet with the Soviet delegation at their embassy. Our delegation, headed by then-Secretary of State Cyrus Vance and former Governor Averell Harriman, met them at their building, decorated Kremlin-style—plain, somewhat severe. Through our interpreters we exchanged pleasantries and a few remarks of substance also. I say "through our interpreters" because I don't believe anyone in our group spoke or understood Russian, but most of the Soviet delegation, including Foreign Minister Gromyko, spoke and understood English. It may appear to be a minor matter, but it gives "the opposition" in any such dialogue additional time to prepare for the proper reply. I wish I could enter a vigorous debate on the floor of the House with those kinds of odds stacked in my favor! And yet what took place in New York City between our two delegations occurs in similar meetings over and over again (and not just with the Soviets), with Americans unable to communicate directly.

A shortage of competent translators and interpreters heightens the problem, and the inadequate pay they receive reinforces the shortage. Little that is published in the Soviet Union is translated into English. Publishers are further discouraged by the knowledge that there are few readers and few buyers for books in translation. It is often said that because ours is an open society, the Soviets can learn more about us than we can about them. But it is not the closed Soviet society alone that is the major block to our understanding. Our own society closes its eyes to what it could read. The All-Union Center for Translation of Scientific and Technical Literature and Documentation in Moscow, only one of several translation agencies in the Soviet Union, reports that its translation output doubled between 1970 and 1973, increasing by 150 percent between 1973 and 1975, or a total of some 350 million words. In addition, the Chambers of Commerce and Industry translated 230 million words in 1975; Intourist translates about 17 million words, and the Central Research Institute for Patent Information, a little over 7 million words every year.

Royal L. Tinsley, president of the American Translators Association, says—in contrast—of the National Translation Center at the John Crerar Library in Chicago, that despite efforts to eliminate duplication and reduce costs, National Science Foundation funds for the center "were cut off a few years ago and the NTC staff was reduced from 11 to 4. Over the past four and a half years the NTC has deposited or reported availability of 85,891 technical translations, but even more were deposited with or reported to the NTC—the staff of four simply could not process any more." The center estimates that no more—and probably less—than half of U.S. technical translations are reported to the center, due at least in part to lack of funds and staff. Tinsley calls it "a national disgrace." [8]

I met a second-echelon Soviet leader, Sergei Kondrashev, in Belgrade, Yugoslavia, where he served the Soviet Union at the Helsinki Agreement follow-up sessions, and I served the United States as a delegate. When I attended the UN session in New York, we had dinner together and he met my family. I speak no Russian but he speaks excellent English. He is a warm human being with deep concerns about the future of the world. We have talked frankly with each other, and, as a result, I believe he understands our political system better, as I am more culturally enriched myself by having become more knowledgeable about the Soviet political process. Such friendships could help me some day. The public image of leaders is that they weigh all the facts carefully before making decisions. Sometimes they can do that. But more often they are thrust into situations where they have to make decisions quickly—not on the basis of a set of facts their staff carefully accumulates for them, but on knowledge and impressions they have accumulated through the years. Because Sergei Kondrashev acquired a knowledge of English I may some day make decisions about the Soviet Union with a little more knowledge, a little more understanding.

Language is a key to opening minds and attitudes. To speak, read, write, and understand another language is the beginning of understanding other people. If we do not understand others' dreams, hopes, and miseries—if we live in a narrow, closeted world—we will fail to elect and select leaders who can take us down the difficult pathway to peace. Leadership cannot be too far ahead of those who follow or it is no longer leadership. A self-centered uninformed public is unlikely to choose those who will make the hard decisions necessary for building a solid foundation for world peace and justice. As one historian has written, "If the ordinary American wants to know who shapes fundamental foreign policy, all he has to do is look into a mirror." [9]

Vietnam is the classic example of the failure of such understanding; 56,226 United States service personnel lost their lives, many times that number were wounded, and perhaps three million Asians died. The immediate dollar cost to the United States was approximately $135 billion. We are paying for that war in many other ways today. Inflation has been caused in part by Vietnam, a consequence of President Lyndon Johnson's understandable dread of proposing tax increases to pay for that war. Additional national debt from that war will require interest payments for the rest of our lives. An even greater price was the division and bitterness and cynicism and grief that grew out of the Vietnam war.

We can learn some lessons from that tragic conflict, the need for specialists who understand what is happening in every corner of the globe; the need for citizens who can read, write, speak, and understand all major languages. The loss in Vietnam came not because of deficiency in military equipment or in the fighting force, but because of deficiency in understanding. There is little evidence that we have learned those lessons.

At the same time that the U.S. military budget rises, support from private and public sources for foreign-area university studies has declined.[10]

Decline in Dollar Support for University Foreign-Area Studies, 1965–72 to 1975–76

Asia	−36.4%
Near East	−44.5%
Africa	−49.0%
Latin America	−60.7%

• Indonesia with 140 million people is the world's fifth most populous nation, strategically located, and rich in natural resources. There are only 127 students of the Indonesian language in higher education in the United States; only six to ten of those will become fluent.

• When the Angola crisis developed, only two Americans had substantial knowledge of that country.

• In vital Kenya, only one of thirty-two U.S. embassy officers has been required to speak Swahili.

• In Somalia, a turbulent and stragegic spot, no one in the U.S. embassy is required to speak the local language.

The most recent report by the General Accounting Office shows *no* students of the Albanian language in the entire United States; 31 of Rumanian; 4 of Bulgarian; 71 of Thai; and 4 of Burmese.

We seem to believe that if an emergency arises, we can turn on a spigot somewhere and the knowledge and expertise we need will spout forth. There is no such spigot or computer or sudden fount of knowledge. We must begin to "stockpile" language and area resource personnel as we have stockpiled strategic metals.

Twenty years ago Prime Minister Nehru of India told me that the Chinese would not have invaded Korea had the United States maintained diplomatic relations and regular conversation with the Chinese leadership. Now historians are starting to tell us the same thing. Rarely in the history of nations do we find that it did any harm for the leaders and peoples of two nations to talk to one another. The lesson of history is that the dangers almost always exist in not talking.

Two sentences from a respected observer of the foreign and domestic scene tell something about our present status: "The poor quality of teaching foreign languages in the United States assures that few students ever achieve reasonable fluency in Russian, Chinese, Japanese, or most other major languages. . . . Issues of central national concern about foreign areas simply are not being studied." [11]

Another student of our scene has noted: "[Our] isolation goes deeper . . . than our ears and tongues. It is really an isolation of soul. Our ignorance of language keeps us nationally from making the kind of salving contact which ties people together, which enables man to talk to man, and which can in the long run prevent embroilment, misunderstanding, and violence." [12]

The Foreign Service Institute of the State Department and the Defense Language Institute operated by the Department of Defense perform effectively but are severely limited. Languages that should be taught are not. The armed forces and the State Department do not use them as they should. The Foreign Service Institute, for example, offers a two-week area course in language and culture fundamentals for those who are to leave for new overseas assignments. Only one-third of the Foreign Service officers, and a much smaller percentage of secretaries and other support personnel, take the courses.

Both the United States and Japan have a security interest in maintaining good relationships between the personnel of our air bases in Japan and the people who live in those communities. An unpublished thesis by a Harvard student spells out in some detail mistakes we are making. At the Yokota Air Base, for example, there are 5,300 U.S. military and civil service personnel, approximately 8,200 dependents, and 2,200 Japanese civilian employees. One person, a Japanese employee, is the community relations officer and the only person authorized to handle contacts with the six local communities. Virtually the only contact Japanese local officials have with the air base is complaints. This

> suggests to Japanese a lack of concern for the community. In addition, Japanese officials find it unpleasant and uncomfortable that they must take the initiative in most of their communication with the base. . . . Building and maintaining a personal relationship is an indispensable part of official and business relations in Japanese society. Much more so than for the stereotypically "businesslike" American, it is important for Japanese associates to establish a personal tie as a foundation for their business dealings with one another. . . . Business tends to be conducted after working hours over a table in a favorite restaurant or bar rather than over a desk in an office. . . . U.S. forces personnel are unable to provide this sort of personal foundation for official liaison. . . . Even the . . . public affairs [personnel], who in interviews often mentioned the importance of "personal contact" in Japanese society, in practice actually have none. . . .[13]

The author points out that the community relations officer is not an ideal person to handle community relations because he is Japanese. Local officials would like direct contact with the Americans in charge of the base.

> Almost no U.S. military personnel are trained to cope with the Japanese language and culture. . . . This lack of appropriate training and background preparation is probably the most important factor in the lack of personal working relationships in base-community liaison. . . . The maximum extent of background on Japanese society, history, politics, economy and culture under the belts of most public affairs staff members is . . . a general three-hour program of orientation to Japan that is mandatory for every serviceman newly assigned. . . . The only Japanese-speaking persons in the entire

public affairs structure at Yokota [Air Base] are Japanese. . . . The military has no comprehensive program of language training for its servicemen assigned overseas. . . . The language problem is a source of considerable uneasiness and frustration on the part of Japanese officials.[14]

A Rand Corporation report on our international research and intelligence operations notes that data collection "tends to dominate analysis." For good reason: If you don't understand a language and a culture, you simply gather the facts and avoid venturing any opinions on what the facts mean. But our government needs the analysis and not simply more stacks of useless paper. Between 1967 and 1979, the federal expenditure for research on what is happening in the rest of the world was cut in half. The Rand report observes:

> The isolation of the intelligence community from academic researchers, the limited opportunities in government service for direct contact with foreign countries, and the anonymity and bureaucratic fragmentation of the analytical process . . . limit interpretive accuracy. . . . We found a remarkable consensus about the problems of maintaining or improving the quality of the government research on foreign areas.[15]

By comparison with the policy of our government, a ruler of the Holy Roman Empire four centuries ago sounds most enlightened. Charles V is supposed to have said, "A man is worth as many men as he knows languages." [16]

I have mentioned communicating directly with the hundreds of millions whose hopes are few and who yearn simply for a little food and life's basics. There is a tendency to ignore them. We barely know who the leaders of Bangladesh are, for example, and we cannot begin to picture the lot of misery that engulfs most of that nation's humanity. It is so vastly worse than the lot of even the most unfortunate in this country that it almost defies our understanding. We tend to want to hide the unpleasant, as we used to hide the fact that people died from cancer. When we have to deal with Bangladesh, it is so much easier to deal with the government and business leaders, the elite. They speak English. They're clean. They're educated. "They're like us."

I do not suggest that we should stop speaking to the leaders of government and business, to the professionals and the others who are the well-educated leaders in these lands. But when we fail to learn to communicate with those who yearn for something better, we miss an opportunity to communicate with future leadership, and, more important, we fail to know the people of a nation.

Unless we create special incentives for our people to learn Hindi, Urdu, and a host of other languages now almost totally ignored, we invite uninformed decision-making— decision-making that misunderstands the public mood and may hurt the very people we hope to help.

Iran provided an example of our distance from realities in the period preceding the overthrow of the Shah, although we had greater access to opinion there then than we have in most nations of the world. Our access came through students who had studied in the United States, and personnel working for U.S. businesses in Iran, rather than through the U.S. Embassy. Morton Kondracke of the *New Republic* had described the situation well:

> It turns out that only six of the sixty U.S. Foreign Service officers in Iran during the revolutionary year 1978 were minimally proficient in Farsi. . . . The political section contained no one who was fluent in the language for much of the year, until a Persia expert was reassigned in the fall from duties handling African affairs for the State Department's United Nations desk.[17]

But U.S. government personnel were not the only people distant from realities. At the height of the difficulties, 120 news correspondents covered the scene—and only one Western reporter could speak Farsi, Andrew Whitley, representing the BBC and the London *Financial Times.*

The United States did not properly assess the public mood in Iran, and while events there (as of this writing) do not appear to have handed the Soviets a victory or domination over that country, it is clear that the actions taken by that government are a rebuff to many of our hopes. The scenario could have been much different and much better had we been more sensitive, more eager to listen and learn.

Former U.S. Commissioner of Education Harold Howe wrote to me in 1979:

> I can't think of a country in the world with as much at stake in its international dealings as the United States and with less commitment to the knowledge base that undergirds its actions. Both our economic well-being and our security are dependent upon our skill and understanding in dealing with numerous countries we know all too little about, not to mention our desire to help with improving the living standards of less fortunate people.

The world's less fortunate have something to do with our own security. We spend tens of billions of dollars each year to prepare for a possible Soviet attack across central Europe. And until we build a better climate of understanding with the Soviets, there is not much chance of diminishing that expenditure.

Since the Soviet leaders are rational human beings, however, and know the devastation nuclear war would bring— know it better than we do since one out of five Russians was killed in World War II—it is highly unlikely anyone in the Kremlin will issue such an order. It is difficult to quantify what those odds are, but I have heard figures from our top military personnel everywhere from a one out of 50,000 chance that it would happen, to a fraction of 1 percent. No one knows. We dare not dismiss the possibility, but the chance of it happening is remote.

But if hungry, helpless, hopeless people in a developing nation in Africa or Asia or Latin America stir up trouble within a nation in their desire to change their lot, the chances that the Soviets will try to take advantage of that situation are almost 100 percent. Soviet belief in their system of government—plus national pride in being a great world power for the first time—propel them into involvement in one nation after another. The Soviet invasion of Afghanistan understandably aroused world anger, but prior to that invasion by troops, a pro-Soviet regime had come into power in a much more typical Soviet "invasion" by subversion, which did not cause a ripple in U.S. public opinion. These developing nations have people whose language we must understand and whose hopes we must comprehend. While we should avoid viewing every internal struggle in a developing nation in a cold war, East-West framework—and we have a tendency to do that—it is not in our security interest to permit the Soviets to become the new colonial power through our own ignorance and/or indifference.

Such situations are much more likely to develop into a Soviet-U.S. confrontation than is anything on the European scene. Neither side is likely to plan an invasion that would result in a nuclear confrontation, but we could accidentally precipitate one. The greater the communication and understanding with people in these areas, the less likelihood of an accidental flash point explosion.

An illustration of the possibility of accidental conflict—and our own weakness—occurred in southeast Asia early in 1979. In the middle of 1978, the Vietnamese government in a variety of ways indicated to U.S. leaders that they would like to establish normal relations and trade in order to avoid being squeezed into either the Soviet or Chinese camp (interestingly, one of our aims in fighting the war there).[18] The Administration privately favored the idea but felt it would cause problems with Congress and would cause domestic political problems for President Carter. So what they acknowledged to be sound policy was avoided. In the meantime, the Chinese government secured great international prestige when the United States acknowledged its existence, as it should have done thirty years earlier. But we handled the recognition ineptly, some of our leaders talking about "playing the China card" against the Soviets, and notifying the Soviets that we were about to recognize the People's Republic of China only two hours before the public learned about it. The Soviets, engaged in a bitter public relations battle with China, were affronted. China, they decided, had to learn a lesson; and they apparently pressured the Vietnamese into invading China-supported Cambodia. Had we earlier established normal relations with Vietnam, this invasion might not have happened. The Chinese, in turn, invaded Vietnam, "to teach them a lesson." Many felt the Soviets would decide "to teach the Chinese a lesson." Fortunately, the escalation stopped there, but I am reasonably sure some in the Kremlin urged limited military action against the Chinese. Had they prevailed, the limited action could have easily become unlimited, and the world could have been engulfed in a nuclear war from which no nation can escape.

It is essential for United States security to maintain communication with people everywhere. To the extent that we ignore an unknown nation and an unknown people, to that extent we ultimately risk our own security.

Our declining interest in foreign languages unfortunately is matched by declining support of international research and of area studies centers. On March 22, 1978, Dr. Rose Hayden testified in behalf of the American Council on Education before the House Subcommittee on International Security and Scientific Affairs, pointing out that international research funding by federal agencies has decreased dramatically, from

$40.6 million in 1967 to $32.6 million in 1976, a loss of 52 percent in real dollars. Area studies centers' total funding at the nation's universities dropped about 62 percent during this same period.

We are a nation of travelers. One-tenth of our nation goes abroad each year. What a plus it would be for the United States if only one-half or one-quarter of the tourists and students and armed service personnel visiting abroad could speak another language with minimal fluency. Instead of offending people, we would learn from them. The U.S. House of Representatives received this message from its Education and Labor Committee in 1958: "As a Nation we are not prepared linguistically to exercise the full force of our leadership in the building of a peaceful world. . . . America can ill afford to let this situation continue."

We send approximately 456,000 troops overseas, well equipped to use certain weapons. The chance that they will be called upon to use those weapons—happily—is small. However, the chance that they will have an opportunity to use German, Korean, or another language spoken where they will be stationed, is almost 100 percent. Since it is distinctly in our security interest to make friends, why not sponsor an incentive program, perhaps a payment of an additional $300 bonus to anyone who studies the language and passes a minimum proficiency test? That would appear to be a wise expenditure of defense dollars. (The CIA is inaugurating just such a program for itself.)

One of the most effective ways to keep informed about events around the world is to read translations of newspapers and documents. The American Translators Association reports, however, that while about twenty-five colleges have a course or two in translation techniques,

> the only viable, comprehensive training programs that have been added for technical translators are those at the Univer-

sity of California at Santa Barbara (French, German, Spanish), Carnegie-Mellon University (French, German, Russian, Spanish), Stanford University (German), the University of Puerto Rico (Spanish), St. Mary of the Woods College (French, Spanish), and the Rose Hulman Institute of Technology (German, Russian). Most of the students in these programs . . . are not training to become translators—they are future scientists and engineers who want to learn how to read foreign research in their own fields. . . . Of a total 162 students enrolled in five of these programs . . . approximately 60 hoped to become translators. The same five programs graduated twelve students [the previous year], at least ten of whom were employed in non-translation jobs or in positions where their language skills were of only minor importance. In contrast, Canada has eight training institutions for translators and interpreters, and Western Europe has over forty.[19]

After the visit of the Chinese delegation, *The New York Times* editorialized:

The Indispensable Mr. Chi

Chi Chao-chu is hardly a household word in America. Yet Mr. Chi has been an indispensable man. If Teng Hsiao-ping had not brought the former Harvard man from the Chinese Foreign Ministry as his interpreter, his discourse with President Carter might have gone uncomprehended. The United States Government, it turns out, does not employ anyone fully qualified as a simultaneous interpreter from English to Chinese.

That painful condition is the culmination of chronic neglect. Unless complemented by academic training in the history, culture, economics and politics of a given society, the knowledge of its language alone becomes a dull instrument—and practically useless in delicate diplomatic situations. Indeed, the translators at summit meetings have often observed that they cannot properly convey nuance of meaning unless they are familiar also with the private views and policies of the principals. Yet the flow of bright young Americans into foreign-language study has slowed to a trickle. Many of the best university study centers are endangered by lagging support.

In 1972, President Nixon was able to speak with the Chinese leaders in Peking only through their interpreters. Seven years later, the humiliation—and perhaps damage—continues on American soil. Absurd, in any language.[20]

When the Deputy Prime Minister of China visits the United States, we must use his translator, and when the President of the United States visits China, we must also use the Chinese translator. While Mandarin Chinese is spoken by more people than any language in the world, the American Council of Learned Societies claims that only sixty native-born Americans not of Chinese ancestry are fluent in Mandarin Chinese. We have no qualified translators for most of the world's languages in the United States government, an incredible commentary.

If we cannot get qualified people to help us with Chinese and Russian, where do we get translators for Burmese, Tamil, and Urdu—and for the many other languages that right now may seem unimportant but that we ignore ultimately at our own peril?

Edmund Burke once wrote, "Great empires and little minds go ill together." Rev. Timothy Healy, S.J., president of Georgetown University and a strong advocate for a more adequate language program in this nation, paraphrased Burke appropriately: "Great empires and international illiteracy go ill together." [21]

One of the most insightful observers of the international scene, Robert Ward of Stanford University, has written with accuracy: "For better or worse, we will in the future be more dependent and more affected by the policies and activities of other states than has ever before been the case in our post-revolutionary history." [22] He adds: "A nation with only 5.3 percent of the world's population that accounts for 25.1 percent of the gross planetary product and consumes an estimated 40 percent of the world's annual use of nonrenewable resources cannot afford to neglect its capacities for the conduct of effective foreign relations."

On another occasion Ward wrote:

> During my adult lifetime the United States has become involved in four major world or diplomatic crises; with Japan and the Axis Powers in 1941, with North Korea and ultimately with China in 1950, with North Vietnam in the 1960's, and most recently with the still unforeseeable but distinctly ominous consequences of the coup in Iran. In every one of these cases retrospective wisdom and responsible scholarship can make a plausible case that the hostilities and national costs involved could have been postponed, avoided entirely, or substantially mitigated—"Had we but known. . . ." [23]

On January 27, 1958, President Dwight D. Eisenhower sent a special message to Congress on education, and in it he said, "The American people generally are deficient in foreign languages, particularly those of the emerging nations in Asia, Africa, and the Near East. It is important to our national security that such deficiencies be promptly overcome."

That message still must be heeded. As a popular song of a decade ago concluded, "When will they ever learn? When will they ever learn?"

· 4 ·

The Cultural Problem

But [the weakness of] the Moslems [was that they] deprived themselves of the principal benefits of a familiar intercourse with Greece and Rome, the knowledge of antiquity, the purity of taste, and the freedom of thought. Confident in the riches of their native tongue, the Arabians disdained the study of any foreign idiom.

Edward Gibbon, *The Decline and Fall of the Roman Empire* [1]

If English was good enough for Jesus Christ it's good enough for me.

H. L. Mencken

Pointing to a little known part of the Helsinki Accords of 1975 which obligates the signing nations to encourage the study of foreign languages within its borders, Rep. Paul Simon (D-Ill.) is proposing to bribe colleges and universities with tax dollars to expand their foreign language departments. . . . America has come further . . . in 200 years than other nations have advanced in 2,000. We have conquered the problems of travel, disease, construction, have subdued the earth, skies and the seas and caused them to serve humanity. And we did it all without the aid of the metric system or an expensive foreign language education to assuage some politician's inferiority complex.

Editorial in the *Progress Bulletin* of Pomona Valley, California [2]

Pride in a language is easily confused with nationalism or regionalism. Wars have been fought over attempts to impose another language on a people. The bravado of the editorial from the *Progress Bulletin* points to one of our problems: To suggest that we should learn a second language is somehow an insult to our nationhood, to our self-image. If we do condescend to learn a foreign language, it is likely to be one tied to our heritage, therefore a little less "foreign."

One of this nation's most distinguished historians, John Hope Franklin, reflects on such chauvinism:

> At a time when the globe is shrinking and no place is really far from any other, the decline in the study of languages is appalling. School boards join parents, who are cheered on by the student, in raising questions about the relevance of the study of French or Spanish. This at a time when we should be extending language study to include Russian, Chinese, and Arabic in the elementary schools. Our disinterest in languages is a clear reflection of our parochialism that makes it virtually impossible for us to see ourselves as integral parts of a larger unit.[3]

"If English was good enough for our Founding Fathers, it's good enough for me." There are several things wrong with that common sentiment: Some of the Founding Fathers did not speak English; of those who did speak English, many—like Thomas Jefferson, Benjamin Franklin, and John Adams—also spoke other languages, and were enriched and helped by it; many were educated in Europe; and even if in 1776 or 1789, they had all spoken only English—it would not be an adequate approach for the 1980s. The Founding Fathers did not have automobiles, airplanes, sewer systems, electricity, and a host of other things we find of value, but I would not want to abandon these conveniences because of the lack of historical example.

The word *foreign* has an unfavorable connotation in our culture. When we describe something as "foreign to our way of life," we do not speak in a complimentary way of that "foreign" thing. We have a "foreign particle" in our eye; it is an abrasive nuisance. "We shouldn't be helping those foreigners," I often read in my mail. Dr. Priscilla Ching-Chung of the University of Hawaii, an American with an Asian heritage, writes:

> Our peoples had to discard their ethnic heritages, wash away anything foreign, and become reborn in the English language and American culture. This anti-foreign psychology permeates our society to the extent that we view any acknowledgement of world interdependence as a threat to our national superiority. We feel the need to always negotiate from a position of strength and to have other nations learn English and adopt our ways.[4]

A *Washington Post* dispatch from China reports, "A million copies of a government guide to the English language have sold out in Peking." [5] Can you imagine the reverse happening in the United States? But why shouldn't it?

There is an old Spanish proverb: "Spanish is the language of lovers, Italian for singers, French for diplomats, German for horses, and English for geese." That is a *Spanish* proverb. We all have a weakness for whatever builds us up and tears others down. Pride in any culture easily slips into arrogance.

We learn parochialism from early childhood on. Remember the Robert Louis Stevenson poem:

> Little Indian, Sioux or Crow,
> Little frosty Eskimo,
> Little Turk or Japanee,
> Oh! don't you wish that you were me? . . .
> You have curious things to eat,
> I am fed on proper meat;
> You must dwell beyond the foam,
> But I am safe and live at home.[6]

Not only do others have "curious things to eat," they have curious things to say. We unconsciously assume that it is "natural" for people to speak English, and that those who don't are in some way inferior. They—whoever "they" happens to be—ought to learn English; it is not equally obvious to us that we ought to be learning "their" language.

Chancellor Alfred R. Neumann of the University of Houston has put it well:

> Our supposed superiority in human comfort, in our standard of living, in the quality of our lives in this country has all too often been translated into a linguistic arrogance which has allowed us to look down upon others who do not speak as we do. If what we have wrought is so good, let them, those other people, learn about it in our language! From there it is only a small step to the next inference: if these other people do not speak the language of our superior achievements, then they must be inferior to us in other ways. Ergo: why learn the language of these inferior people? [7]

Mark Twain caught this language attitude in dialogue between Huckleberry Finn and his black friend Jim:

> " . . . and some of them learns people how to talk French."
>
> "Why, Huck, doan' de French people talk de same way we does?"
>
> "*No*, Jim; you couldn't understand a word they said—not a single word. . . . S'pose a man was to come to you and say Polly-voo-franzy—what would you think?"
>
> "I wouldn' think nuffin; I'd take en bust him over de head. . . ."
>
> "Shucks, it ain't calling you anything. It's only saying, do you know how to talk French?"
>
> "Well, den, why couldn't he say it?"
>
> "Why, he *is* a-saying it. That's a Frenchman's *way* of saying it."
>
> "Well, it's a blame ridicklous way. . . ."
>
> "Looky here, Jim; does a cat talk like we do? . . . does a cow? . . . And ain't it natural and right for a cat and a cow to talk different from *us?*"
>
> "Why, mos' sholy it is."

"Well, then, why ain't it natural and right for a *Frenchman* to talk different from us? You answer me that."

"Is a cat a man, Huck? . . . Is a cow a man?—er is a cow a cat?"

"No, she ain't either of them."

"Well, den she ain't got no business to talk like either one er the yuther of 'em. Is a Frenchman a man?"

"Yes."

"Well, den! Dad blame it, why doan' he *talk* like a man?"[8]

Former U.S. Ambassador to Japan Edwin O. Reischauer writes:

We would regard with pity and some contempt a foreign ambassador or lesser diplomat in Washington who could neither speak English nor read the *Washington Post.* An American ambassador in Korea who does not speak and read Korean or an American embassy officer in Cairo who knows little or no Arabic should be considered equally incompetent. There is no reason why a country like the United States should be satisfied with that sort of third-rate service in a field of activity that is so crucial to our nation and to mankind's future.[9]

We lose culturally and we lose economically. A long-time observer says, "While multilingual foreigners do part of their work in lobbies, at bars where truth in wine is revealed . . . monolingual Americans feel out-talked and outwitted."[10]

Former Secretary of State John Foster Dulles wrote:

It is not possible to understand what is in the minds of other people without understanding their language, and without understanding their language it is impossible to be sure that they understand what is in our minds. Each language, including our own, is a delicate precision tool of immense potential value.[11]

It is one of the ironic quirks of our culture that it is often more acceptable to plead ignorance than to know. "I don't know anything about poetry, or opera, or foreign languages," is more acceptable in almost any crowd than admitting to knowing them.

As a consequence of such parochialism, foreign news coverage by the U.S. media relies more and more on "stringers," the work of nationals who speak the language. Yet nationals sometimes are not in a situation to provide news stories that reflect unfavorably on their governments. Several years ago, I visited a nation then suffering under a dictatorship, and talked to a United Press stringer who was paid a small amount each month to send wire stories. Was he in a position to write anything unfavorable about the government? "No," he replied, "I would like to, but I have not only myself but my family to think of. An American or British reporter can do that, because at the most, that reporter is removed from the country. I must be careful."

If the Shah is overthrown in Iran, or if Somoza is toppled in Nicaragua, we will provide coverage, but "lesser stories" are often ignored in our self-centered culture. Take the economic problems of Great Britain, for example. We are more interested in a baseball strike or the latest details of a murder than in more substantial news from abroad that will ultimately have a greater impact on us. *The New York Times* notes editorially: "Only a handful of newspapers still maintain overseas staffs. News magazines prefer cover stories on Hollywood graft, cuisine minceur and sex on television. A recent television special featuring Henry Kissinger, foreign policy's only superstar, won absymal ratings and stirred up only the Harvard faculty." [12]

A second reason we rely more and more on stringers is the decline in the number of daily newspapers in the United States: When the *Chicago Daily News* folds, so does the *Chicago Daily News*'s excellent foreign coverage. Those papers that remain are understandably concerned about making a profit, and foreign news coverage probably does not boost income. In strictly financial terms, foreign news has to be considered a loser. The chain newspapers that are increasingly serving the nation are auctioneers of words, and the high bidder is usually not international news coverage. The nation's need for good international news is greater than it has ever been, yet fewer American correspondents represent the American press abroad than at any time since World War II.

When the media do send a reporter overseas, often he or she cannot speak the language and must rely on an English-speaking person or on persons willing to provide information, frequently inaccurate. Faced with such a choice of information, publishers often choose the less expensive stringer. And media executives, like the rest of us, have suffered from an education that has provided a limited vision of the rest of the world. Insularity breeds insularity.

Better foreign news coverage will come when we who are readers and viewers and listeners expand our own interests to include the rest of the world, and demand better foreign news. Part of that acculturation process is through learning another language.

Cultural isolation has an adverse impact on the nation's lawmaking. We are one of the few countries in which lawmakers are criticized for traveling abroad.

No one denies that abuses have occurred in legislators' travel, but the fact is that members of Congress travel too little, not too much. Members of the House and Senate can boast in their districts about no trips overseas, and gain votes doing it. Yet anyone who makes that "boast" is in fact confessing that he or she is not doing the job properly.

I have yet to see an editorial in any newspaper anywhere that criticizes a member of the House or Senate for insufficient travel. Yet some of our mistakes in foreign policy are well-intentioned actions by House and Senate members who simply do not understand. There is no substitute for being in a country, and talking to the people (through interpreters in most cases, unfortunately).

After World War II, the United States spent almost 3 percent of its national income (GNP) helping the hungry and desperate beyond its borders. No nation in history has responded as generously. But a generation later, we are spending less than three-tenths of 1 percent of our GNP to combat poverty abroad, far less in percentage than Japan and most of the nations of Western Europe. After World War II, House and Senate members could come back home and tell their constituents, "I'm helping your relatives in Germany and France and Italy and elsewhere." There was political mileage in helping hungry people. But today the people who need help live in places like Bangladesh and Mali and Guatemala. They have few relatives in the United States. There is no political mileage in helping them. Even Americans who find themselves in Bangladesh, miss some of the sense of agony and heartache if they cannot speak to the people there.

A congressman can get cheers when he or she delivers a speech denouncing foreign aid. When we cannot communicate with the developing nations, we are less likely to send food and help. A world of peace and stability becomes more remote.

Evidence of our cultural isolation is everywhere. Ambassador Reischauer recalls one example:

> Not long ago there was a magnificent television series about the Western Christian artistic tradition. I personally enjoyed it very much. But it had for me one deep annoyance. Its title was simply *Civilization,* as if the Western Christian tradition were the whole of human civilization. Repeatedly it made mention of those outside this tradition as barbarians threatening to snuff out "civilization. . . ." That this title seemed at all acceptable for the historical presentation of only a single cultural tradition shows how sublimely ethnocentric even our sophisticates can be. No wonder the school boy accepts with-

out question the "our gang" approach to the human experience.[13]

The head of the Berlitz Company observes:

> I have heard . . . that in Europe, Europeans, because of their
> exposure to foreign languages, are more inclined to learn
> another language than Americans. I would accept this excuse
> if I could apply the same reasoning to Japan or Brazil to
> choose two isolated countries. . . . Anyone who has been to
> both countries will agree that percentage-wise you will find
> more Japanese who understand and can speak another lan-
> guage than you will find in America. The same applies to
> educated Brazilians.
>
> Another observation we can make is that when a European
> learns a foreign language, he believes in learning it well. . . .
> When a German tells you he speaks French, he means just
> that: *he speaks French.* If you want to switch to French in the
> middle of the conversation and continue in that language,
> that's fine with him because, as he has said, *he speaks French.*
>
> When an American tells you he speaks French, it often
> means a lot less. He may mean that he *reads* French, or simply
> that he knows enough French to order a meal in a restau-
> rant.[14]

We learn both little things and big things through the
nuances of language. We smile and laugh and cry at our mistakes and those of others. And when we learn another language we catch those subtleties that cannot be transferred.
How do you explain *gemütlich* to someone who does not
speak German? The simple pleasure you receive from being
able to communicate, to visit another country and be able to
buy your railroad tickets, or ask questions about a menu, or
ask directions—these are self-enriching experiences. Foreign
language knowledge also brings an appreciation of music,
reading, cooking, gardening, dance, and movies. And, as
Richard Brod has observed, there is a "transfer effect
between learning about a 'foreign' culture and learning to

understand the culture of a domestic minority or ethnic group." [15]

Joseph Conrad, who wrote several of the finest novels in our language, grew up speaking Polish and learned English in his twenties.

One of the best language teachers in the nation, Professor Marta Bret of the University of North Carolina at Charlotte, says she believes that, wisely used, language and travel open

> your mind. I find that when I don't travel for a while I get set in my thinking—my ideas start to petrify—I start thinking my ways are right; I'm not opening my mind to new ideas. The right type of foreign language exposure has the same impact as travel. Ideally it should be combined with travel. But even without travel a properly taught language course opens minds to new ideas and a new culture.[16]

We learn through others whether or not we are getting our ideas across. And sometimes we are surprised. When Louis Agassiz, the Swiss-born writer and geologist, applied for U.S. citizenship, he was asked, "Do you advocate the overthrow of the government of the United States by force or violence?" He thought for a moment and then said, "By force." [17] He thought we expected him to choose one.

There are less humorous examples in any large American city. In a typical incident, a policeman questions a youth in English; a frightened Spanish-speaking youth does not understand and starts running, and the policeman fires. To help meet such problems, the most widely known foreign language teacher in this nation, Dr. John A. Rassias of Dartmouth College, invited twenty-six members of the New York City transit police to a two-week session at Dartmouth to study Spanish, using his own dramatic techniques. Four Puerto Rican police officers who assisted as instructors spent three twelve-hour days learning Greek under the Rassias method—to prove to them that a great deal can be learned in another language in a short time. The idea for the program came from a Dartmouth senior, Dean Esserman, who had studied French under Rassias. He had seen the need for a police emergency medical rescue unit. One day it suddenly struck him: "How do you service a community you can't talk to?" [18]

One writer refers to the United States as "a linguistic wasteland." [19] Despite our rich ethnic mix, and despite the fact that we are the fourth largest Spanish-speaking nation in the world, we remain ignorant of languages and cultures other than our own. Though we now have 19.8 million foreign visitors a year—far more than most nations—we provide few signs in other languages. Athens, Tokyo, and thousands of other cities around the world have signs and announcements in several languages in airports, bus terminals, and museums. Why can't we? Shouldn't we require our Capitol guides to learn to speak other languages—also White House tour guides and Kennedy Center guides? Instead, we convey cultural arrogance. *Time* magazine tells of reactions from French tourists in the United States: "Because no one seems to speak their language, they conclude that no one likes the French." [20]

Part of the explanation for our "linguistic wasteland" is our geography. We are the only nation in which you can travel 3,000 miles and hear and read and speak only one official language. We have not been invaded since 1814; we are surrounded by oceans and by two friendly nations, one of which is predominantly English-speaking. As one observer notes: "The Mexicans we ignore; the Canadians we scarcely recognize as foreign." [21] But, despite the geography, there are reasons for hope. Americans tend to be friendly and gregarious; we like everyone—and we may come to the point when we want to communicate with others in their own language. There are encouraging signs. A survey by the University of

Michigan's Survey Research Center shows a receptivity to foreign languages. Among their findings: [22]

• Three-quarters of our population believe languages should be taught in the elementary schools.

• Ninety-two percent believe a foreign language should be offered in junior high and high schools.

• More than 45 percent of the population would like to learn a foreign language, and 20 percent would like to learn two languages.

• Of those who have studied a foreign language at any point, more than three-fourths felt it worth the effort. In this group, 15 percent felt that it led "to better awareness and understanding of people from other nations"; a slightly smaller number felt it helped them communicate with people they know; 13.5 percent said it helped them in English; 11 percent found it useful for travel, and 6.5 percent reported it helped them on their job or helped them get a better job.

• Eighty-four percent of those with children sixteen and under would encourage their children to take a foreign language.

• Seventy-three percent expect that their children will have the opportunity to use a foreign language.

• Seventy-four percent believe knowing a foreign language "would help Americans to have a better awareness and understanding of people from other nations."

• Forty-one percent believe a foreign language should be required in grade schools, and 47 percent believe it should be required in junior high or high schools; 40 percent believe it should be a college graduation requirement.

I find these statistics encouraging. There is no massive groundswell of support for a more adequate foreign language program, but there is not only no hostility, but a public readiness to avoid continuing as "a linguistic wasteland."

Another encouraging and little-noticed plus is the Peace Corps. Peace Corps returnees come back with a greater sensitivity to people in other countries, and with language skills learned in a practical setting. Among the languages taught by the Peace Corps as this book is written are Swahili, Sesotho, Chichewa, Guarani, Dari, Arabic, Fijian, Gilbertese, Korean, Malay, Nepali, Tagalog, Pidgin, Thai, Tongan, and Yemeni Arabic. As the countries that request Peace Corps volunteers change, so do the language requirements. But hundreds of Peace Corps personnel are studying languages few Americans have ever studied, and both the host country and our nation are richer for this interest.

There is a widespread belief in the United States that acquiring another language is a special "gift" that some people have and that most people do not have. The Berlitz method of teaching (discussed in more detail in Chapter 8) was started in the United States and is now a worldwide enterprise, but in only one nation do they need to provide an initial free lesson as bait—their country of origin, the United States. Elsewhere it is assumed that all people learn basics in a foreign language just as they learn fundamental skills in "reading, writing, and arithmetic." But Americans are still convinced that some outside force—God, Mother Nature, call it what you will—has given a chosen few the talent to speak in other languages. George Bernard Shaw once wrote, "No man fully capable of his own language ever masters another." [23]

Author-philosopher-physician Martin H. Fischer commented: "Any man who does not make himself proficient in at least two languages other than his own is a fool. Such men have the quaint habit of discovering things fifty years after all the world knows about them—because they read only their own language." [24]

In a wide variety of ways all people are coming closer to one another in what some have aptly called "a global village." I recall the day some years ago when in a hotel room in Tokyo, I dialed the hotel operator and told her I wanted to place a call to the United States. "You can dial that directly from your room," she replied. In less than a minute I found myself talking to my children in the United States.

Professor Stephen K. Bailey of Harvard writes:

> I am always amazed by "100% Americans." They sleep in Hong Kong pajamas, drink Colombian coffee, turn on Japanese TV sets, drive to work in a VW Rabbit from Germany, turn on lights and air conditioning powered by Arab oil, wear shoes made in Italy, eat a chocolate sundae whose cocoa beans come from Ghana, sip Scotch and sodas, eat Polish salami sandwiches, wear Swiss watches.[25]

My teenage children like the music of a singer whose musical skills somehow escape me, and suddenly I discover that the same nonmusical sounds are popular in Moscow. The Levi's of the United States are popular in Uruguay, and the split skirts of the Orient are a part of our own culture.

The multinational corporation is a growing phenomenon. Symbols for automobile traffic (like no left turn signs) and behavior (like no smoking signs) are becoming more international. How a car is built in Sweden has an impact on air pollution in southern Illinois. Religious and political beliefs are less and less limited by national borders. Organizations are international: Rotary International, Lutheran World Federation, even the Boy Scouts and Girl Scouts are international organizations. The trend toward internationalization and interdependence is clear.

Some say, "English is now the international language." And there is *some* truth to that. English is the only official language of almost thirty nations and one of the official languages in sixteen. But increasingly, technical journals are appearing in other languages; in part because of the knowledge developing in other countries, and in part, because of language nationalism. The present trend will continue for technical publications. And *a decreasing percentage of the world's popula-*

tion speaks English. One study shows that when a U.S. scientist or scholar "is faced with work in a foreign language which he cannot read, he generally ignores the work or seeks some kind of substitute in a language that he can handle." [26] If we believe we can effectively trade, provide political leadership, keep on top of scientific developments, and share the benefits of the cultural growth of the rest of the world in our island of English, we fool only ourselves.

A small item in the publication *Translation News* tells a little about our cultural status: "During the 1977–78 year there has been no meeting of the National Translation Center Advisory Board." [27]

A Georgia school board member approached Genelle Morain, who teaches language education at the University of Georgia, and asked, "Why should a student who will never leave Macon, Georgia, study a foreign language?"

She replied, "That's *why* he should study another language!"

· 5 ·

The Bad News from Our Elementary and High Schools

In general, I am of [the] opinion, that till the age of about sixteen, we are best employed on languages: Latin, Greek, French, Spanish.

Thomas Jefferson [1]

As far as languages are concerned, this age [five] is so supple, that within a few months a German child learns French unknowingly while doing other things. Such learning is more effective when carried out in the earliest years.

Erasmus [2]

I wrote to all of the nations with embassies in Washington to ask about their foreign language programs: Seventy-six nations responded, and among them, none can compare with the United States in neglect of foreign languages.

Because school systems vary so much from country to country, comparisons by grade level, or by elementary and high school level, are difficult. Comparisons of commitment, however, are not difficult.

The following is not a comprehensive survey of language study in these countries, but I believe it is the most complete study published to date.

Nation	Description
Afghanistan	English, French, and German are required, starting in elementary school.
Arab Emirates	English is required from fifth through twelfth grades. The last two years of high school are divided into two streams, literary and scientific. Those who are in the literary stream must take another foreign language, usually French.
Argentina	Elementary system is divided into two categories, and in one, a foreign language is required, starting in the third grade. High schools require a foreign language all five years, three years of French and two of English, or three of English and two of French.
Australia	Some public schools have foreign language requirements, most do not. Where there is no requirement for foreign languages, the states provide training availability at the elementary and secondary level, including Indonesian, Japanese, Chinese, Dutch, Spanish, French, Greek, German, Hebrew, Latin, Czech, Hungarian, Latvian, Lithuanian, Polish, Serbo-Croatian, Turkish, Ukrainian, Italian, Malay, and in the state of Tasmania, Esperanto is also available! Enrollment percentages are more than double those of the United States.

Nation	Description
Austria	For admittance to a university, eight years of a living foreign language plus four years of Latin are required. Before age ten, there is no requirement for a foreign language but courses are "very popular." Of children ten to fourteen, 75 percent receive instruction all four years in at least one foreign language. For ages fourteen to eighteen, about 25 percent receive four years of instruction in at least one living foreign language and, in most instances, Latin also.
Bahamas	Spanish and/or French is required during the first three years of high school.
Barbados	Spanish is actively promoted by the government as a second language.
Belgium	Foreign languages are compulsory in some areas from third grade on, throughout the country from fifth grade on. Foreign language is compulsory throughout secondary school (ages twelve to eighteen). A second foreign language is available from third grade on, a third foreign language available from fourth grade on.
Benin	There is no foreign language requirement in elementary schools. Two foreign languages (English and a choice of Spanish or German) are required in the secondary schools.

Nation	Description
Botswana	Setswana, the national language, is used for the first four grades, and English is taught. From grade five on, English is used as the medium of instruction.
Brazil	There are almost no foreign languages taught in the elementary schools. English is taught in all three years of secondary school. University entrance examinations require the knowledge of foreign languages.
Bulgaria	From fourth grade through high school, Russian is taught; from eighth grade on, English, French, or German. Students graduate from high school with two foreign languages.
Burundi	French is required in elementary schools. French and English are required in secondary schools and at the university level.
Cameroon	French and English are required from elementary school through the university level. "Faculty of the university are obliged to be bilingual and deliver lectures in either of the two languages. Medical school graduates are expected to present their final dissertations to an international jury in their first language, a summary in the other, and answer questions from the jury in the language in which it is asked." [3]

Nation	Description
Canada	An important post in Canada is Commissioner of Official Languages. Because of the language question in Canada, stress is placed on learning French in English-speaking areas and English in French-speaking areas. Immersion is gaining in emphasis. Not only is language training stressed in the schools, but also for adults.
Central African Republic	Sango and French are taught in elementary schools. In the secondary schools and universities, French, English, German, Spanish, and Russian are available.
Chad	French and Arabic are taught in grade schools. German, Spanish, and English are taught in high schools and universities. Russian is optional.
China [4]	Foreign languages are stressed. In urban areas, three years of primary instruction and five years of middle school are provided, fewer in rural areas. Radio broadcasts are used extensively for foreign language instruction.
Cyprus	English is required both in elementary and secondary schools.
Denmark	Starting in the fifth grade, six years of a foreign language are required, a second is optional.

Nation	Description
Egypt	Starting in the sixth grade, six years of English are required; in the tenth grade, three years of French.
El Salvador	A foreign language is required in secondary schools. In order to graduate from a college or university, students are required to show proficiency in a foreign language.
Fiji	English is required both in the elementary and secondary schools.
Finland	In the comprehensive schools (ages seven through fifteen), the first foreign language starts in the third grade and the second starts in the seventh grade, both required. Sixteen hours per week are spent on the first, seven hours per week on the second. It is possible to study two *additional* foreign languages before graduation from high school.
France	Sixth grade through secondary school, one foreign language is required. Ninth grade on, a second foreign language is required. For entrance into college, students must pass at least one foreign language examination.
Germany (East)	From grade five on, for six years, Russian is required. From grades seven through ten, a second language (usually English or French) is optional.

Nation	Description
Germany (West)	One or more foreign languages is generally required at some point in what would be the equivalent of our elementary or high school.
Great Britain	About 5 percent study a foreign language in elementary schools. From age eleven, 85 percent study for three years, 40 percent, four years or more.
Greece	It is common to study a foreign language at elementary level but not required; one foreign language is required at secondary level.
Guatemala	Foreign language study is voluntary at elementary level, required at secondary level.
Guinea-Bissau	Portuguese is required in elementary schools. Both French and English are required in secondary schools so that, by graduation from high school, all students have had three foreign languages.
Haiti	English and Spanish are required in secondary schools.
Honduras	Five years of a foreign language are required.
Hungary	In grades five through eight, Russian is compulsory, another language optional. In high school, Russian and one more foreign

Nation	Description

language are required, a third optional. They also have a series of specialized foreign language high schools. At the university level, two years of Russian and two years of another language are required. Fluency in another language is required for Ph.D.

Iceland

Danish is required from age ten for six years. English is required from age twelve for four years. In *menntaskoli* (last two years of high school, first two years of college), Danish is required for two years, English for four, and either French or German is also required. Other languages can also be taken.

India

All students are required to study two languages other than the mother tongue.

Indonesia

One foreign language is required in elementary school, one in junior high school, two in high school, two in university.

Iran

Seven years of foreign language are required, starting in the sixth grade. At the university level, six "units" out of 120 needed for graduation must be in a foreign language.

Ireland

It is not required but "the majority of students do study a foreign language during the course of their education." French is optional in elementary schools.

Nation	Description
Israel	English is required from grades four or five, through twelve. Arabic is being encouraged as a second foreign language. All schools in the Arabic section learn Hebrew from grade three. English is required in the university unless the student passes an English proficiency test.
Italy	Foreign languages are required in high school, optional at elementary and university levels. Most popular language is French, followed by English.
Jamaica	Foreign language study is limited at elementary level, "fairly universal" at secondary level. Students must pass a foreign language examination to be admitted to study humanities at university.
Japan	Although foreign language study is technically not required, more than 80 percent of Japanese students take foreign languages starting at the age of twelve. Two foreign languages are required for university graduation.
Jordan	English study is required from the fifth grade through university.
Kuwait	In grades five through ten, eight forty-minute classes a week in English are required. Grades eleven and twelve are divided by course; either English or French is required.

Nation	Description
Lebanon	One foreign language is required in elementary school and secondary school. Two foreign languages are needed before graduation from college.
Lesotho	The government requires that classes be held in English, so that all students learn at least one foreign language.
Liberia	Knowledge of French is required for high school graduation, and is taught in grades eight through twelve.
Luxembourg	In elementary schools, German and French are required. In secondary schools, English and either Latin, Italian, Spanish, or Russian are required.
Madagascar	French is required at elementary and secondary level. For university graduation, written and oral tests must be passed in English, German, or Spanish.
Malawi	English is required from third grade to university.
Malaysia	Foreign language is required either from first grade or fourth grade, depending on the area, through twelfth grade.
Mali	Foreign language is required in secondary schools.

Nation	Description
Malta	Maltese and English are taught from first grade. In secondary schools, students must study Arabic and one other foreign language. Proficiency in English and one other foreign language is required for university admission.
Mauritania	Students start studying French in second grade. English is compulsory in secondary school.
Mauritius	English is compulsory at elementary, secondary, and university levels. It is the official language, though the population is largely French-speaking. Other languages are available as electives.
Mexico	Primary schools generally offer a foreign language. Study is required in secondary schools. Student must pass a foreign language examination to get a university diploma.
New Zealand	At the secondary level, those who take the pre-university courses usually take two or three years of a foreign language. Those who attend vocational schools are much less likely to.
Niger	Two foreign languages are required in secondary school. Before entering university, students must pass examinations showing an ability to read and understand two foreign languages.

Nation	Description
South Africa	"Every elementary school child is required to learn at least two languages." Two foreign languages are required in secondary schools, a third is optional.
South Korea	In grades seven through twelve, English is required; in grades ten through twelve, another language is also required. At university level, English is required all four years.
Spain	Foreign language is required in elementary and secondary schools.
Sri Lanka	Foreign languages are required from grade one.
Sudan	There is no elementary instruction, but English and French are required for three years in secondary schools.
Sweden	By graduation from secondary school, students have nine years of English, and two-thirds of the students have either French or German from grade seven on.
Switzerland	A second Swiss national language must be started in the fifth or sixth grade. A foreign language (or a second language) must be begun in the seventh or eighth grade and continued through secondary school and university.

Nation	Description
Syria	In intermediate and secondary schools, all students must take five to seven hours a week in a foreign language, usually French or English.
Taiwan (Republic of China)	English is required from seventh grade on. A second foreign language is required in college.
Togo	Two foreign languages are required at the secondary level.
Tunisia	French is required in elementary school, and a second foreign language is required in high school.
Uganda	"English is the official language while Swahili is the National language." Mastering English is stressed and required.
U.S.S.R.	In a ten-year school system, almost all take at least one foreign language in high school; one foreign language is required in university; a second or third foreign language is required in graduate school.
Yemen	Foreign language study is required in secondary schools. Knowledge of a foreign language is required for college or university graduation.

Nation	Description
Yugoslavia	From fifth grade through high school, a foreign language is required. A language examination must be passed for university graduation.
Zaire	French is required in elementary and secondary schools. Other languages are optional at secondary school and university levels.

Problems in foreign language study occur in other nations than our own. Although Australia has placed greater emphasis than we on foreign language study, a recent Australian magazine noted:

> Our schools show a sharp fall in the number of students learning foreign languages. . . . Does it really matter if our children study only English? If Australia is to continue its increasing involvement with the rest of the world, and within our own region in particular, then from a national point of view it matters very much indeed. . . . If the opportunity arises for your son or daughter to learn a foreign language, give it careful thought. . . . You may be widening future career options.[5]

Great Britain also has reported a drop in foreign language study, particularly in Asian languages; and Germany, a decline in the study of a *second* foreign language.

A hidden reservoir for increasing our use of foreign languages is the pool of young people for whom English is a second language. The aim of bilingual education, however, has not been to preserve a significant part of our heritage, but to teach non-English-speaking youngsters how to read, write, and speak English, to "mainstream" them (to use one of those new and overused words of educationese). We have not effectively assimilated these young people; we have viewed their presence in our communities as a liability rather than as the asset it is. We have segregated them during their bilingual education years without acknowledging it; and because they are isolated, they acquire English slowly.

When the bilingual bill offering federal aid for teaching English to those with other first languages first passed, the law stated: "In no event shall the program be designed for the purpose of teaching a foreign language to English-speaking children." With the help of my colleagues in the House and Senate I was able to change that. The old law reminded me of Theodore Roosevelt's 1919 statement: "We have room but for one language here, and that is the English language, for we intend to see that the crucible turns our people out as Americans and not as dwellers in a polyglot boarding house." [6]

Yet children learn a language better from each other, not from teachers. We are gradually noting the obvious, that when we put together a class of fifteen Spanish-speaking children, for example, and ten non-Spanish speakers, they learn from each other. Both sides are enriched. And, as one of the most prominent educators of this century, Dr. James B. Conant, has noted, "There can be no question that children learn foreign languages more readily when they are young." [7]

Estimates vary, but there are probably about 30 million people in this country whose first language is not English. About 12 million of these are Hispanic; about 3 million, German; 3 million, Italian; sizable numbers, French and Polish; and many others are from the Orient.

Not many decades ago, it made little difference if an immigrant Swede learned English or not; there were many unskilled jobs that could use his muscle power. But in a day of automation, unskilled jobs that demand no language skills are few. English is necessary. Still, our aim should be not to stamp out every vestige of the heritage of those who speak another language, but to permit it to enrich our country. Those who speak another language have a right to be proud of their heritage, and they should understand that we want to share in it.

By recognizing the resource of our foreign language community, we will be able to learn from them. Through them we can extend a hand of friendship to people in other countries whose view of Uncle Sam has not always been good.

Bilingual education continues to engender fear and misunderstanding. The Spanish-speaking population, some predict, will become the largest minority within the nation by the end of the century. Will we be headed toward Quebec-style seclusion? As statehood for Puerto Rico moves closer to becoming a possibility, and as the numbers of Spanish-speaking people within our borders grow through immigration and high birthrates, fears will increase. Good bilingual programs will help to resolve the problems and quiet the fears. Puerto Rico as a state—should the people of Puerto Rico vote that way—will enrich our culture and diversity, not detract from it.[8]

One possible alternative to bilingual education has been tried and it has failed. For a long period, a form of "forced immersion" dominated the Southwestern United States. Any use of Spanish was forbidden, even on the playground. It resulted in a high drop-out rate and friction between Hispanic and Anglo sections of a town. Similar punitive programs compelling Native Americans to speak English have led to serious problems. We now have moved to voluntary immersion and bilingual classes for several years as an interim period of adjustment. Problems remain: For example, some bilingual teachers are not genuinely bilingual; they lack either English-speaking ability or Spanish-speaking ability.

Bilingual education might be termed "modified immersion." The principal aim of bilingual programs will continue to be the acquisition of English-speaking skills. The immersion programs are aimed at conveying language abilities other than English through the entire curriculum.[9]

A 1957 survey of Illinois high schools found that, among 562 students responding, most took a foreign language course because they needed it for college or because their parents advised it (more than one reason could be listed): [10]

College entrance requirements 300
Wishes of parents 296
Influence of homeroom and other teachers 110
Advice of school counselors 103
Influence of principals 78
Miscellaneous 21

But today only a few colleges still require foreign language for entrance. For all practical purposes, the first student motivation has been eliminated. It is still true that some schools, Duke, Stanford, and Northwestern, for example, all other things being equal, prefer a student with some foreign language background. A Northwestern newsletter to school counselors stated:

> The College Faculty has identified two competencies that we believe all of our students should possess, although we know that not everyone admitted here does indeed possess them. The first of these competency requirements is the ability to write coherent prose in English; the second asks for proficiency in the use of a foreign language.[11]

But the primary motivating force—college entrance—has been drastically diminished. The second motivating force, wishes of parents, has also weakened. Washington, D.C. experienced a flurry of attention when City Council Chairman Arrington Dixon took his children—ages ten and eight—out of public school, sending them to "a private school where they will be able to learn French." [12] But this is an exception, particularly in the high school years and beyond them. Whether for good or bad, parents do not dominate the decisions of their children as they once did. What motivated students yesterday to take a foreign language course apparently will motivate few students today. Those of us who sense a great national need must recognize the necessity to find new ways to motivate. The old answers aren't good enough.

The American habit of moving makes the problem worse. One of every five Americans moves every year. A third-grade student who is in a French-emphasis program in Montgomery County, Maryland will be unlikely to find a French-emphasis program in the fourth grade, no matter where the family goes—there are only six such programs in the nation.

It is difficult to plan kindergarten through high school for a student as a European school system might. Still some exposure to language is better than no exposure—despite the suggestion made by the distinguished Harvard president and educator James B. Conant that anything less than four years of a foreign language before college is worse than nothing. I don't agree; to learn even one year of a foreign language is to learn something about another culture. If every high school could be persuaded to offer a four-year program, I would probably not settle for less; but high schools are *not* so persuaded. One year's exposure to a language is better than none.

Most high school students who sign up for foreign languages take them for one or two years. Indeed, most schools offer no more than two years.

Large high schools should be encouraged to provide third (and fourth) year language programs.

A small high school may not be able to provide the third and fourth year of all languages, but every school should provide these extra years for at least one language.

If only half the schools with two-year language programs would expand them to three-year programs, that in itself would be a substantial step forward. In Dr. Conant's famous 1959 study of American high schools, he used four indices to measure the academic worthiness of a high school. One was whether or not it offered three or more years of a foreign language.

"We can't have a language program without cutting back on something else," I can hear some school administrators and board members saying. "We need new band uniforms and better lights for the football field." Sometimes difficult choices have to be made.

Winston Churchill High School in Potomac, Maryland has 1,800 students. More than 1,000 of these are enrolled in foreign language courses, taught by ten teachers (more than in many universities). It is the largest high school foreign language faculty in Maryland and probably one of the largest in the United States. The head of the program, David Roos (who is Dutch by background; his wife, Mexican), considers foreign language study "basic to the curriculum. Every student should take a foreign language."

More than 500 students in Winston Churchill take Spanish, more than 300, French, and more than 100, German. Four levels of Latin are offered, six of Spanish, five of French, four of German. A variety of activities stimulates interest, including a nine-day trip to Spain in the spring for those who can afford it. The major problem is class size: Several have more than thirty students, the smallest has sixteen.

A less traditional program is operated by Hillcrest High

School in the borough of Queens, New York City. Of the 3,000 students, more than half sign up for one or two foreign language courses; 100 students are enrolled in the School of International Studies, "an interdisciplinary program involving the English, foreign language and social studies departments." The principal describes the program:

> Three periods per day students meet with specialists . . . to study in depth the history, culture, politics, economics, literature, religion and language of several areas of the world. The course is developed as a world tour during which time the students take a vicarious trip . . . to become saturated in every aspect of a particular area of the globe.[13]

Students intern at importing firms, travel agencies, or international business councils. Those who take the courses in international studies are in the upper 20 percent of their class.

Foreign language instruction faces many obstacles, among them the money crunch and the understandable new emphasis on basics. I discuss the money problem later in this volume. The emphasis on basics assumes that foreign language is a luxury, not a fundamental; yet one of the most effective ways to get students to understand, read, and write better English is the study of another language. The basics issue may work against foreign language instruction temporarily but ultimately it must support it.

A concerned Nevada teacher handed me clippings from the Reno newspapers reporting that school authorities had decided "that high school students should have more English, math and world history and less electives." [14] Foreign languages are an elective there, in almost all schools. School Superintendent Marvin Picollo of Reno, Nevada is quoted as saying, "I know some people consider elective courses sacred—mainly those who teach them."

Such cynicism notwithstanding, every study I have seen

shows that foreign language study does not detract from other skills, and, generally, in a measurable way, improves them. One of these studies, of sixth-grade pupils in the public schools of the District of Columbia, found consistent, measurable improvement in English after Latin, Spanish, or French study. The study of the nation's educational problems headed by Willard Wirtz found that, while SAT (Scholastic Aptitude Test) scores are showing general decline, foreign language students maintain relatively higher scores. The other major test in the nation, the American College Test (ACT), shows the same. A computer study at Southern Illinois University of a carefully chosen sample of 7,460 students who had taken the ACT tests indicated that those who take foreign languages tend to get the best scores; study of a foreign language raised scores in all categories, particularly English; students who were not in the top one-fourth of their class gained more from the discipline of a foreign language than did the top one-fourth.[15]

Wall Street Journal columnist Vermont Royster observes: "Students going to college are deficient in language skills. Some still are when they leave. That is indeed appalling, and it's long past time we raised some hell about it. Language is the tool for learning anything, and there's no better way to sharpen it than to hone it on some tongue other than your own."[16]

In Albuquerque, New Mexico, one group of fourth- and sixth-graders received intensive Spanish language instruction for six months, a second group, none. The results on the California Test of Mental Maturity "given at the beginning and at the end of the study indicated that the experimental group made a significantly greater gain."[17]

Imaginative, creative communities can help themselves in many ways. Take Marion, Illinois, as an example. Marion is a city with a population of 13,000 in the rural southern part of the state, an area with high unemployment and other major economic problems but an area of great beauty and much potential. Suppose the school board, the mayor and city council, and some of the other "movers and shakers" of Marion decided that the city should build more bridges to the rest of the world. They agree, for an experimental decade, to offer Japanese in elementary schools and four years of Japanese in the high school. Exchanges are worked out with Japanese teachers.

So far as I know there is not a citizen of that area who is of Japanese heritage. Marion would be doing something unusual, which would make news, not only in the United States but in Japan. The educational system would be enriched, students would have more job opportunities, a new culture would be opened to them, and eventually, when a Japanese manufacturer is trying to determine where to put a new plant, he might very well decide to put it in a community that has demonstrated a cultural sensitivity to the Japanese.

I am not proposing this for Marion, because a community has to make such a decision for itself. But there are thousands of communities like Marion around the nation, and there are many nations in addition to Japan that would welcome such a cultural tie. Communities are like individuals—they get ahead if they are willing to risk a little, work a great deal, and use some imagination.

Although I took three years of Latin and one year of classical Greek in high school and recognize that they helped me, when my daughter faced a choice of taking Latin or a modern language, I encouraged the modern language. I may have been wrong.

The Los Angeles Unified School District, adapting a Philadelphia program,

> by using classical Latin, improved the English language arts skills of youngsters in grades 5 and 6 who were reading below grade level. . . . The statistical results of the experimental/

developmental phase of the Language Transfer Project support the long-held intuitive hypothesis that a Latin program, appropriately designed, can and does improve English language skills and motivates students to continue the study of languages other than English.[18]

If the same talented and enthusiastic teachers taught Spanish or French, would the same improvement in English language skills have occurred? I don't know. Austria, alone among the nations as far as I know, continues to place heavy emphasis on Latin.

Whether students should be encouraged to study the ancient, classical languages or modern ones is a judgment call, with most of those discussions in recent years tilting in the direction of modern languages.

Novelist Kurt Vonnegut, reflecting on his background, said:

> I didn't learn until I was in college about all the other cultures, and I should have learned that in the first grade. A first-grader should understand that his culture isn't a rational invention; that there are thousands of other cultures and they all work pretty well; that all cultures function on faith rather than truth; that there are lots of alternatives to our own society.[19]

Cultural education and the learning of languages should begin sooner than they now do in the United States. Foreign language training is rare, immersion in foreign languages even rarer. Canada, on the other hand, now has elementary school immersion language programs in nine of her ten provinces. Not only do these students pick up another language, but they do not slip back in knowledge of the mother tongue or in any other subject. Perhaps the most carefully evaluated U.S. program has been the grade school French immersion program operated by William M. Derrick and the Comprehensive Educational Center of the State University of New York at Plattsburgh. The experience has had a strongly positive outcome.

An experimental program with 386 Munich, West Germany kindergarten children showed that, with only thirty minutes of exposure to French a day, the children learned to use about fifty French words in a simple grammatical form. "Most astonishing of all was the side-effect of learning French—the way it helped these children in their use of their mother tongue."[20] Native French speakers were used, with no translation back into German. Teachers told stories in French, like Little Red Riding Hood, that the children knew. Such a program is clearly achievable in almost any school district.

Students who have had foreign language exposure in grade school are more likely to take a language in high school than students without this background. A Harvard University study of language majors in their senior year of college showed that "on the average, students who started [their language studies] in the elementary school were distinctly superior [in foreign languages], at graduation from college."[21]

A woman from Sylvania, Ohio, who read of my interest in foreign languages, wrote to me:

> We wait too late to teach languages in our schools. Children in the second, third and fourth grade are interested in learning another language. . . . I speak from experience. As a child I spent a lot of time with our next door neighbors. They spoke only Italian. Until I married and moved away from the East, I spoke Italian as fluently as English.[22]

A wise counselor is former U.S. Ambassador to Japan Edwin O. Reischauer. He writes:

> There is one . . . basic educational reform I would put forward as having relevance for the development of a sense of world citizenship. This is an increase in language study . . . a key

element for producing a sense of world citizenship. . . .
Foreign language instruction should come early in the educational process, basically at the elementary level. This is because it can serve as a fundamental shaper of the child's perception of the world. It can help him accept the fact that there is much in the world that differs greatly from what he sees around him. . . . It should come early also because the young child learns a foreign language with ease and pleasure.[23]

· 6 ·

Colleges and Universities—
A Mixed Picture

Institutions with the name "university" can be spearheads of provincialism.

Francis X. Sutton [1]

There are other forms of culture beside physical science; and I should be profoundly sorry to see the fact forgotten, or even a tendency to starve, or cripple, literary or aesthetic culture for the sake of science.

Thomas H. Huxley [2]

At no time in the educational history of this country has mastery of a modern foreign language come to be recognized as the hallmark of a well-educated man or woman.

James B. Conant [3]

Collegiate language programs need to be more multidisciplinary, and less literature-oriented.

Eisenhower College in Seneca Falls, New York describes itself as "the small college with the global perspective." I have never been there but I am impressed by what I read and hear. It has a stronger language program than many state universities. And its offerings in this field are fairly typical of the strengths and weaknesses of language programs today. Here is their choice of Spanish courses:

102

Beginning Spanish I
Beginning Spanish II
Individual Instruction
Intermediate Spanish I
Intermediate Spanish II
Advanced Grammar and Composition
Advanced Grammar, Composition and Introduction
    to the Techniques of Literary Analysis
Introduction to Spanish Literature I
Introduction to Spanish Literature II
Literature of the Golden Age I
Literature of the Golden Age II
Literature of the 19th Century I
Literature of the 19th Century II
Literature of the 20th Century I
Literature of the 20th Century II
Spanish Civilization
Latin American Civilization
Selected Topics in Spanish (in the Field
    of Literature)
Individual Study in Spanish

That is an above-average program, but increasingly, the Spanish student will not only want to have background in nineteenth-century literature, but also learn accounting and engineering terms in Spanish, and the Spanish of the hotel business and the field of chemistry. Of all the courses in language offered at Eisenhower, one, "Scientific German and Technical Reading," is the type of course that must increasingly appear in college catalogs. Language study must become more contemporary, more career-oriented. Florida A and M University, a school which has not put great stress on foreign languages, for example, has modified its curriculum to recognize the importance of bilingual employees to tourism income for Florida, and particularly to help those who may be involved in tourism-related fields.

Even at the high school level, some schools are experimenting with more applicable language instruction. At Live Oaks High School in Morgan Hill, California, a student can take a course in "Airline Stewardess's German" or "Secretarial Skills in German." At Manchester Community College in Connecticut, Dr. Toby Tamarkin, language department chairman, has created courses like "Career Spanish," with lessons on hospital admissions, credit procedures, income tax and accounting problems, and secretarial and office procedures. Dr. Tamarkin reports that both students and faculty are enthusiastic about the new emphasis. Universities should seek a language tie-in with the engineering school; "Spanish for Pharmacists" should be of interest to an increasing number of pharmacists in this country. Language is not only a tool for diplomats and a hobby for the country club set. Two obvious needs—among hundreds that could be mentioned—are lawyers who speak Spanish and lawyers who speak Japanese. Are our language schools and our law schools cooperating? Unfortunately, the answers are not encouraging.

The Board of Regents of the Florida University System took steps other states would be wise to take. It employed consultants to evaluate their strengths and weaknesses in the field of foreign languages. One comment of the consultants could apply in almost any state:

> The opportunities for the foreign language community to relate to the bilingual needs of businessmen and government officials involved in the expanding trade efforts of Florida are obvious. The consultants, unfortunately, detected little recognition of these opportunities in the thinking of those responsible for the development of foreign language programs.[4]

It might be added that the University of North Florida offers no language courses whatsoever!

The University of North Florida is not alone. There are a number of colleges and universities without foreign language offerings, and some have to struggle to keep a program. Typical of these struggles is Castleton College in Castleton, Vermont, population 2,720. Castleton, with 1,300 full-time students and 1,000 part-time students, is the largest of five state colleges. The only languages taught are French and Spanish. I spoke at a meeting at nearby Dartmouth College, and in the audience was the entire foreign language faculty of Castleton—both of them! After my remarks, they told me that the board of trustees had under consideration a proposal to reduce the foreign language faculty by half. I took the liberty of asking for the name and phone number of the chairperson of the board, and called and talked to her. I am pleased to say she was not unsympathetic, and the board decided—probably unrelated to my call—to keep both faculty members, a minor victory, though no one could call a two-person faculty at a state college an adequate language program.

The picture is not all bleak. There are signs of hope here and there, institutions aware of our academic deficiencies. Harvard is among them. And because Harvard has adopted a core curriculum, which will be fully implemented by 1983, including a "Foreign Languages and Culture" requirement, it is probable that other schools will follow Harvard's leadership. Harvard's aim "is not merely to avoid an exclusive focus on Western traditions but to expose students to the essential and distinctive features of major alien cultures, whether Western or non-Western." [5]

Another place of good news in the field of foreign language study is Washington State University at Pullman, Washington.

The Washington State University program is headed by a

Frenchman, Jean-Charles Seigneuret, who has "enormous energy, considerable administrative ability, and a flair for salesmanship." [6] He and his faculty believe their program is important, and they actively promote it among faculty and students. Although the registrar is not happy with that practice, all incoming freshmen are contacted. An amazingly wide array of language offerings is available. Intensive summer workshops are offered in French, German, Spanish, and Japanese. Double majors—in a foreign language and another field—are encouraged. Enrollment in foreign languages has, as a consequence, increased by 50 percent since 1970.

Wherever you find a school like Washington State University going so clearly against the trends, inevitably there is some one person who has shown leadership. When asked why Winston Churchill High School (mentioned in the previous chapter) has such an outstanding language program, the answer I received was: "The enthusiasm of David Roos," who heads the program. There are other outstanding leaders: John Rassias at Dartmouth, Gerd Schneider at Syracuse University, William M. Derrick at Plattsburgh, New York. When one person understands the importance of the cause, and is willing to communicate that to his or her colleagues on the faculty and to others, a program can succeed; but where an attitude of defeatism and submission to a massacre of the foreign language program exists, you expect nothing more than a continued diminution of the program.

Here is other "good news":

• Southern Illinois University has developed an honors program, initially to be a multidisciplinary look at Asia, Africa, and Latin America.

• More business schools are adding some type of international dimension requirement for their majors and graduate schools.

• St. Edward's University in Texas is taking a look at the third world as it develops its academic programs, hoping to combine internships in developing nations with academic offerings.

• The University of Iowa is dividing its French Department into four tracks for French majors, literature being one of the four tracks, with students required to take something in each track. The result encourages the multidisciplinary approach to the language.

• At William Paterson College in New Jersey, foreign language enrollments are up more than 300 percent in the last four years.

Under a contract with the federal government, Harvard undertook a study of the language attainments of foreign language majors in their senior year of college. The results of the 2,784 seniors studied included: [7]

• "Much poorer in listening and speaking skills than they were in reading and writing." In listening and speaking skills they were in the "limited working proficiency" rating on the average, while in reading and writing they moved up to "minimum professional proficiency."

• Students who were willing to participate (51.4 percent did) had a higher grade average than those who did not, suggesting that the actual average for college senior language majors is not as good as this study.

• "Students at private institutions scored significantly higher, on the average, than students at public institutions."

• There was an association between foreign language proficiency and the level at which studies started. Those who started in elementary schools did the best.

• The majority of foreign language majors are women: 84 percent of French majors; German, 59 percent; Russian, 62 percent; and Spanish, 75 percent. But there were no testing differences between the sexes.

• Use of a language laboratory did not show any significant effect.

• When a language is used in a home it helps appreciably.

Dr. Barbara C. Dease, head of the Department of Modern Foreign Languages at Jackson State University in Mississippi, outlines some problems from her perspective:

> Where the funding of the institutions of higher learning is apportioned reluctantly by legislators who exhibit [an] anti-intellectual and anti-ethnic bias, we educators in Mississippi face a never-ending task of making do with little or nothing. . . . I know of one university which has eight faculty members who handle a three-language undergraduate and graduate program. I know of a university which would not allow a foreign language department to apply for an NEH [National Endowment for the Humanities] consultancy grant because of fear of an outsider coming in to assess the weaknesses of the department. I know of a foreign language department in a public school system whose instructors are so demoralized that they had no student participation in the National French and Spanish Contests. I know of a college board which must give permission to each faculty member who wishes to travel abroad. I know of a Southern state which has no outlets to show foreign films, because they are regarded as "subversive" and "detrimental to the mores and morals of its citizens." I know of a state university system which has no doctoral degree in any foreign language. I know of a state where state and national language associations have little or no impact on the training program for high school teachers of foreign languages. I know of a state where the state coordinator of foreign languages is also the coordinator of English.[8]

In many ways the nation's community colleges are the most exciting frontier in the field of higher education. Over half of the first-year college students of the nation attend community colleges. They are a major educational force in most states, providing an opportunity for hundreds of thousands who would otherwise be unable to get an advanced education. A community college education is handy; it is cheap; it is not elitist; it reaches adults not otherwise involved in higher education. But one of five community colleges offers no foreign language courses, and of those that do, most report low attendance. There often is not much encouragement. About 3.6 percent of the community college students enroll in a foreign language class; only 29 percent of two-year college instructors at any point in their careers travel abroad, a much lower percentage than at four-year institutions.

A survey of community colleges in Massachusetts in 1977 reported:

> If the international studies educational goal is to give a smattering of information to a few students, this is achieved by the present system. . . . If the goal is to reach the general student population, this is simply not being accomplished nor is it being considered by most of the community college personnel. The potential to reach a sizable number of the general population served by the community college system is there, but it is not being realized.[9]

The College of San Mateo in California, a two-year college, offered a course in "Survival French" for travelers. Forty-five enrolled. Soon Spanish, German, and Japanese were added. And these courses stimulated interest in the more traditional language courses. This particular story does not have an immediately happy ending—budgetary restrictions forced the dropping of the courses along with all other noncredit courses. But the head of the department, Henry Cordes, says, "We've demonstrated there is a real demand for foreign languages. Community colleges that identify and meet it can extricate themselves from their presumed predicaments."[10]

An even less happy ending—so far—has come to the program at Bronx Community College in New York, where enrollment in languages dropped from 2,548 in the fall of 1975 to 1,319 in the fall of 1978. The foreign language faculty sent a letter that explains this tragedy:

> This decline of 48% is due not to lack of student interest but to budgetary cuts which have catapulted a large and active

modern language faculty of fifteen part-time and twenty full-time persons to one of no part-timers and only fifteen full-time members. Since three of these full-timers are on leave . . . [the] teaching load has increased by about 50%. . . . This 50% increase is not in the number of classes taught by each instructor but in the number of students in each class. Where twenty-five students in a course used to "close" it for registration purposes, the tally now runs in most classes to thirty-eight and over. Compare these figures with the maximum recommended by the Modern Language Association, fifteen to eighteen, and you will realize the extent to which language students are being short-changed.[11]

The College of Lake County in Illinois opened in 1969 with 900 students and one French teacher. Ten years later, with enrollment increased by more than 10,000, the college still has one French teacher.

A substantial bright spot in the two-year college picture is the national leadership they have selected. President and chief executive officer of their organization Edmund J. Gleazer, Jr. says:

We're interested in foreign languages and international education because we're trying to qualify people to live effectively in the world of today. If they are to make decisions as citizens, they need a better understanding of the realities on which to base those decisions. . . . International meetings I attend discussing adult education I think are significant because neither in their country nor in ours are we dealing with an elite, as too many of our programs do. Community college and adult education programs are important because they are reaching a different and increasingly important audience.[12]

We cannot expect our colleges and universities to do what our elementary schools and high schools have not done. But we can expect leadership to meet our national needs if the first two units of our school system fail us. One way of meeting these needs is study outside of the country. An American may study abroad. But a foreign student studying here can also help to teach us.

Travel has been a story of opportunities seized, and opportunities missed. How many students and faculty members travel abroad each year on a not-for-credit basis? No one knows. But we do know that there are 250,000 foreign students—three out of four of them men—enrolled in postsecondary education in the United States, approximately 2 percent of our total student enrollment. We have more students from other countries than any other nation, though our percentage is far lower than Canada (16.9 percent), or France (12.4 percent), for example.

Of the 250,000 foreign students in the United States, more than 40,000 are in community colleges, 3,400 of these in one college, Community College in Florida; 63 percent are in public colleges and universities. Eight in ten came here to study on their own finances, or with the help of their government, but with no U.S. financial help. These students could help us learn. About one in three or four of all foreign students studying abroad study in the United States. Eleven percent of doctoral candidates here are foreign students. Foreign students bring approximately $1 billion annually into the U.S. economy. They could also bring us their language and culture if we would let them. Yet at the same time, U.S. support for student and faculty exchanges abroad is declining. Kibbey M. Horn, director of International Programs for the California state college and university system, reports that of 12,000 full-time faculty members in that state, in 1979, only 20 were involved in faculty exchange programs. And as support for exchanges has declined, the proportionate number of students coming to the United States from the world's poorer nations—the nations that need the training the most—has also declined.

"The less affluent United States students wanting to study

abroad have less of an opportunity than at any time since World War II," says Wallace B. Edgerton, president of the Institute of International Education.[13] Some believe that the improved student loan programs and the improved grant programs for a student from a family with limited income can reverse that trend, particularly if personnel at colleges understand how this can work and encourage it. The Basic Economic Opportunity Grant program can be used for overseas study if the student is enrolled in a U.S. institution with an overseas program. The money cannot be used, however, if the student is actually enrolled in a school in another country. But within these limits, the BEOG program can be helpful to a student whose family meets the income requirements. However, the financial barriers are growing, in part because of the depreciation of the dollar. The average overseas academic year program for an undergraduate in 1973 cost approximately $3,000, but by the 1979–80 school year, the cost has reached $10,500—out of reach for most students.

This deficit is compounded by the reality that a relatively small percentage of our black students have studied any foreign language, making them less likely to be offered the chance for study abroad. Leaders in the exchange field agree that the lack of foreign language preparation of students limits the usefulness of travel and study abroad. Blacks are less likely to take foreign languages because they are most likely to attend elementary and high schools that do not offer them; they are most likely to be counseled against taking a foreign language, and are more likely to attend a collegiate institution that neither offers nor recommends foreign language instruction. The reason often given by counselors for not encouraging foreign language training for blacks is "weak English skills." Foreign language training could help overcome the English deficiencies; where foreign language is not taught, English may not be taught well either.

Professor Louise J. Hubbard of the University of the District of Columbia may well be correct in suggesting that an aura of elitism and even racism has surrounded foreign language study in the United States, and that some people who feel that if foreign languages are difficult for whites, languages should not be recommended for blacks.

Whatever the cause, the result is clear. A 1976–77 study showed that 3 percent of bachelor's degrees in foreign languages went to blacks; of 3,147 such master's degrees, 99 went to blacks; of 752 foreign language doctorates, 14 went to blacks.[14] It is hard to disagree with an unpublished dissertation that "the black graduate must be better, not less prepared, than his white counterpart if he is to move out of monolingual and monocultural isolation."[15]

As our college-age population decreases, many colleges have difficulty maintaining their numbers and their financial base. In their eagerness to enroll students, a few schools have actively solicited abroad, accepting students not academically prepared for a U.S. college, and in some cases offering little in academic enrichment to these students. The extreme example is Windham College in Vermont, which tried to save itself with Iranian students. Ultimately the school folded, leaving these Iranian students stranded. Foreign students would be wise to make sure that the school soliciting them is accredited and that it accepts only those able to benefit. The National Association for Foreign Student Affairs has condemned "indiscriminate recruitment in their homelands of foreign students whose subsequent experience in this country is a waste of their time and money." The experience of some of these students, they said, "greatly diminishes the reputation of U.S. higher education."[16] Schools that do not exercise some caution do a real disservice to this nation.

The diminishing interest in foreign languages in the United States also causes problems with students we send abroad. The binational commissions that advise on Fulbright grants have "noted the increasingly inadequate language preparation of [United States] grantees." They observed "that American professors frequently overestimate the language proficiency of the students they recommend. . . . The standard of language teaching must be strengthened if students are to be able to get the benefits of intensive educational experience overseas." [17]

How effectively are we utilizing visitors to our country? A story from the *Washington Post* tells of Dae Ki Ko, a six-year-old Korean-born first-grader at Glencarlyn Elementary School in Arlington, who told his mother that he felt "alone" in his new life in the northern Virginia suburbs. To cheer him up, she invited two dozen of his classmates to a party for her son.

On the big day, two children appeared at the Ko house.

"Dae was so sad. It was so hard for him to understand what happened," said a friend of the family. . . . These foreign-born children feel like perfect idiots when they know they are not. They feel so isolated and alone." [18]

Confronted with the daily task of obtaining a basic education in a language they often cannot read or understand, the children of these new immigrants often face bitter emotional adjustments.

The University of Pennsylvania sponsors a program it calls "International Classroom." For $15 it will bring a graduate student from another country into a high school classroom, community college, or any school or organization making a request. Hosts and their guests from abroad are both enthusiastic about the program. Other colleges could do the same.

Studies of reactions of foreign scholars to their experiences in the United States frequently show, as a Fulbright exchange study showed, that our guests "would have been willing to talk to people outside their immediate circle of acquaintances but didn't know how they could arrange it." [19]

Sweden has an unusual policy on foreign students. Any

student from Denmark, Norway, Iceland, or Finland—described as "Nordic" students—can register on exactly the same basis as a Swedish student. Since there is a sizable Swedish-speaking population in Finland—Swedish is one of two official languages of Finland—there are approximately 6,000 Finnish students in Sweden. Sweden reserves 10 percent of openings in institutions of higher learning for other foreign students. In 1979, about 50 American students were enrolled in the Swedish academic program.[20] However, only about 1 percent of our college students go abroad to study.

We have come a long way since Georgia passed a law stating that any student who left the United States to receive "an education under a foreign power" for three or more years could not, when he returned to Georgia, "hold any civil or military office for an equal number of years." [21] Still, few programs exist to encourage travel for study. The improved loan and Basic Economic Opportunity Grant programs may help to send more students abroad.

Host countries, however, are reluctant to place an American student into Oxford or Heidelberg or any other institution, if the American student will be taking the place of one of their own students, and at a considerable cost to the taxpayers of the host country. Most nations do not charge, as we do, for collegiate training, and most allow a small living stipend as well. To alleviate this problem, Georgetown University in Washington, D.C. is experimenting with a trade; a student at Georgetown pays tuition, room, and board at Georgetown, then trades places with a student from another country. Illinois State University has worked out an exchange program with Nanzan University in Japan to send ten to fifteen students to ISU, and the same number from ISU to Nanzan. The University of Massachusetts at Amherst has reciprocal student exchanges with universities in Africa, Europe, and Asia, bringing more than fifty students to that school from universities abroad.

The University of Illinois reported in 1979 that 32 percent of their faculty had "significant foreign experience" compared to 55 percent in 1966.[22] A 1977 report for the Carnegie Council on Policy Studies in Higher Education notes that "the proportion [of faculty] spending time abroad has declined." [23] International education scholar Barbara B. Burn says, "If in the course of a forty-year career, every American faculty member was able to spend one semester abroad every ten years, this would require a fivefold increase in the numbers abroad each year." [24]

There are efforts to stimulate study abroad. The Institute of International Education puts out two catalogs, one for summer study, for credit, abroad—900 programs—and the other for the regular academic year—763 full-year programs. College libraries should have these catalogs, or they are available from IIE at their home office, 809 United Nations Plaza, New York, New York 10017 ($6 for each catalog). The American Institute for Foreign Study, 102 Greenwich Avenue, Greenwich, Connecticut 06830, sponsors or assists in academic programs, and educational travel programs abroad (in which high school students can participate), some for no more than one week. American Institute for Foreign Study, a for-profit corporation, sponsors about 12,000 students a year for language-learning or education programs abroad. Nonprofit organizations that sponsor students abroad include Experiment in International Living, Youth for Understanding, and American Field Service.

There are some—former Ambassador Reischauer among them—who believe that exchanges among high school juniors and seniors may be even more valuable than exchanges among the colleges and faculty because the high school level students are considered to be more open, more eager, more adaptable, less set in their ways. Yet, there are only about 9,000 foreign students in our high schools at any one time, compared to about 250,000 at the college level.

Two-thirds of the high school visitors are sponsored by the American Field Service (founded as a volunteer ambulance corps during World War I) and Youth for Understanding. These students live in homes, not dormitories. Their taste of American life is much more typical than that which the college student receives.

There are about 2,000 American students at the high school level in other nations (out of a total U.S. high school enrollment of 14,300,000), the same two organizations accounting for about three-fourths of these.

Maria Elena Gonzalez has just returned to Uruguay after her senior year in high school. She lived in our home. It was a grand experience for us, and I trust for her also. We learned about Uruguay, and her hometown of Salto in particular. In hundreds of little ways we learned about differences and similarities in traditions and outlook. Incidentally, when Maria came to the United States as a high school senior, she spoke her mother tongue, Spanish, had some understanding of Portuguese, and had studied English for seven years, French for three, and Italian for one.

One of the problems with college exchange programs exists at the high school level also. Like college students, those high school students from abroad tend to come from wealthier families. A broader base of participation would give us more accurate insights into other countries, and would include many countries that now ignore the exchanges as luxuries they cannot afford.

The barrier of language prevents more effective use of the exchange faculty in the United States as well. S. Frederick Starr has written:

> It is far more likely that a student at a major institution abroad would hear an American lecturer than it is that an American student would hear a foreign lecturer. This fact may be attributed in good measure to problems of language. . . . The

overwhelming number of those Americans lecturing abroad present their wisdom in the English language.[25]

An American lecturing abroad can usually find a fair number of students who understand English. But a teacher from abroad lecturing at an American university in Spanish or French or German or Russian would have a much more difficult time.

The Department of Education provides grants to U.S. citizens to teach abroad at secondary or primary schools or attend educational seminars. This is a good concept but has been allowed to drift. It needs improvement and more support. Like many other programs, it has too much of a European cast. Of the 352 grants for the school year 1976–77, 347 were for Europe, 5 for East Asia and the Pacific, none for Africa or Latin America or Eastern Europe. Of the 131 teachers actually placed in 1978–79, 100 went to the United Kingdom. That is imbalance. A second imbalance is the U.S. location of the teachers. For 1978–79, 47 percent of the teachers came from five states: California, Pennsylvania, Virginia, New York, and New Jersey. While eleven states each had one person, California had forty-six. Illinois had three. Wisconsin, North Carolina, and Tennessee, among others, had only one. The concern is not "we ought to get our share," but rather that there should be an equal opportunity for teachers in all states.

The Fulbright-Hays program involves about 650 American college scholars a year, 0.001 percent of all U.S. college faculty. While federal funding has remained fairly constant in absolute dollars during the past decade, inflation has caused a precipitous decline in value received.

Other problems have been summarized by a University of Illinois faculty group:

> In attempting to keep the number of awards constant, the grants have become too small to attract the best people. . . .

> The program operates in a way that is rather clumsy, resulting in severe delays. ... A top-level person from the United States has long-term obligations, and she/he cannot simply be given a month's notice ... at least a six-month notice is needed. ... The whole system of decision-making is too complex. ... This program must become more attractive to professionals—lawyers, journalists, social workers, [and] businessmen.[26]

The problem of foreign languages in postsecondary education is a problem of numbers in that fewer than 10 percent of all college students are required to have a record of having studied a language or having a competence in one in order to get into a college, and fewer than one-fifth of all college students (by the most generous estimate) ever receive any foreign language instruction. But it is also a problem of allocation: Spanish, French, and German (in that order) are the most commonly studied languages. But we also need people who are fluent in Russian, who can read and write and speak the languages of the other Soviet republics; students with a knowledge of Japanese and of Chinese; more students who know Arabic, Hindi, Urdu, Indonesian, Portuguese, Swahili, and the dozens of significant languages of the lesser developed countries that are moving up economically, or that are in a strategic position, either geographically or politically. We ought to have some citizens who know every existent language or dialect.

In part, we meet these needs through a series of programs of international studies at our universities. The relatively few dollars invested in these studies have been among the best investments this nation has made in recent decades. But the programs have these weaknesses:

1. *They tend to be too broad in coverage.* An "African Studies Program" sounds impressive, and one or two may merit such a title, but how many universities can really provide an indepth study of all of Africa? The Horn of Africa, maybe;

north of the Sahara, perhaps; Nigeria, a huge task in itself. Programs that pretend to cover all of Africa or Asia or Latin America or some other region are often skin-deep.

2. *Some down-play language skills.* It is possible under some programs to get a Ph.D. in an area of international studies and not learn anything of the language or languages of the area. This sounds incredible, but it is true. A study by Richard Lambert shows that 79 percent of the faculty in international studies programs never travel abroad for professional reasons. The Lambert study notes: "More than half of the graduates of [international studies] centers have taken no language training at all, while the training for others was the average equivalent of about 4½ semester course units." [27] In some cases, there is no academic tie, either formal or informal, between those who teach languages and international studies.

3. *They have developed without a pattern, with inadequate relationship to national need.* The present international studies programs grew up almost by whim. Someone at a school felt a need or saw an opportunity to start a particular program, and with the okay from the school administrator, and perhaps some foundation funds, a program was launched. But no one—to this day—has asked the fundamental questions: What areas are we covering and what areas are we not covering? And how adequately?

4. *They are financially weak and getting weaker.* Much of the funding for these programs has come from foundations. Foundations have had to cut back as the equity market, which has been their financial base, has declined. Also, foundations usually prefer to initiate programs, not to sustain them year after year. And the foundations, like the U.S. public generally since the late 1960s, have shifted more attention to domestic concerns. The foundations devote about 2 percent of their total expenditure to international education. The biggest contributor, the Ford Foundation, from 1951 to 1973

averaged $13.3 million annually in support of international education programs, but in 1978, less than $4 million. Ford's initiative, leadership, and foresight provided substantial international preventive medicine. But it believes that, fundamentally, international education should be a government responsibility. Ford is right. The federal government provides about 10 percent of the funding now, the balance provided for the most part by state governments and the universities. When the average annual total support for the major area studies programs for the year 1965 to 1972 is compared to the support for 1975–76, and allowance is made for inflation, the result is, by region: South and/or Southeast Asia, down 50.9 percent; Near East, down 68.8 percent; Africa, down 71.3 percent; Russian and East Europe, down 64.4 percent; Latin America, down 77.6 percent; East Asia, down 63.9 percent.[28] A statement of the American Council of Learned Societies summarizes the situation well: "As private foundations have for all practical purposes stopped supporting foreign area studies and the government has picked up only some of the pieces, the individual facilities are one by one succumbing to financial malaise and the network in general is in deep financial trouble." [29] The present level of funding is an invitation to fewer and fewer programs and weaker and weaker programs. The funding commitment should also be for periods of perhaps five years, so that stronger programs can be planned.

5. *Some are academically weak.* Library support is often lacking. A special problem of some complexity, the inadequacy of funding for library materials, comes at a time when there is a mushrooming of available material, much of it essential for adequate research and much of it important to the foreign language student who wants to understand not only a language but a culture. We cannot pretend to have good international studies programs if we have inadequate library support, a fact easily overlooked when dollars are allocated. Also

international studies faculty is sometimes weak. Schools that do have programs should make sure they are giving their students substance.

6. *They do not involve enough institutions.* Harvard, Yale, Cornell, and Stanford have excellent programs of international studies, but we have yet to evolve a plan for a community college in New Mexico, an historically black college in Louisiana, or a small state college in Nebraska. Not that the Nebraska school can or should duplicate the Harvard program, but a degree of specialization would permit the small school to contribute significantly—and to benefit.

I have one other concern with international studies programs. No school should believe it is fulfilling its global mission to the students on a campus through such programs, for they reach only a small percentage of the student body. International studies programs are of great importance to the nation, but they are not a substitute for an integrated campus effort to teach world sensitivity. International studies programs can be part of that campus endeavor, but never more than part.

In 1977, Robert Ward of Stanford wrote what is a fitting close to this chapter:

> Educational systems by their very nature tend to be conservative. . . . As a consequence, school systems usually lag considerably behind the real state of knowledge and contemporary affairs. In quieter and less competitive times, we could afford this lag without too serious cost. But one cannot help but wonder if this is still the case.[30]

· 7 ·

The Quality Problem

Some years ago I received a letter from a mother whose son had taken two years of high school Spanish, and received straight *A's.* When he entered the University of Illinois, he was not admitted to an advanced class. They advised him that he had learned almost nothing in those two years of Spanish. When I chatted with the principal of that small high school, he told me that the teacher had only limited knowledge of Spanish. He was primarily a mathematics teacher.

123

This is an isolated instance, but a 1967 Harvard study of college senior foreign language majors found: "College senior populations exhibited clearly higher mean scores in foreign language skills (except speaking, in some cases) than did samples of foreign language teachers at NDEA Language Institutes." [3] This is both good and bad news, suggesting that the teaching level is not high in secondary schools, but that some of the future (and present) teachers may do a little better.

One authority on the comparative role of schools internationally, Torsten Husén, notes: "In the United States, where French at the high school level as a rule is taken for only two years, the level of competence achieved is rather dismal." [4]

The International Institute of the University of Dallas, deciding to determine what corporations were looking for in students with a Master of Business Administration degree, found that businesses regarded international exposure as "valuable" and language fluency as "important." The institute's director, Dr. H. A. Merklein, undertook to "improve the linguistic ability of our graduate M.B.A. students." Dr. Merklein recalls:

> It seemed obvious at the outset that the B.A.-holder in foreign languages would be our prime candidate. However, it soon became apparent that most foreign language majors with a B.A. degree are not fluent enough. . . . They could not sit at a negotiation table to discuss contractual arrangements or the purchase or sale of a given merchandise. . . . The other day I had a student enroll in our M.B.A. International program. Her major was French. When I learned this, I asked her a very simple question in French, namely, that surely she must speak French well with her degree in French. The answer coming back to me in English was, "I see I have to pursue my study of French some more." [5]

The State Department established the Foreign Service Institute because, as its director says, "It became apparent that few colleges and university graduates had speaking competence which approached the standard we felt necessary in any foreign language." [6] An overseas observer of the brief flurry of foreign language teaching in elementary schools here after Sputnik noted: "One cardinal feature . . . is the role of learners in drilling their classmates, for in many cases, the class teacher is as ignorant as his pupils and he learns along with them." [7]

A Rand Corporation survey found "both business and government [leaders critical of] . . . American language training institutions for frequent failure to train people well in spoken languages as used in business and government work." [8] An unpublished Ford Foundation report notes: "The principal obstacle to the development of first-class competence in the foreign and international field is the low level of language teaching in the United States." [9]

There is another perspective.

Cynthia Parsons, education editor of the *Christian Science Monitor,* has written more about foreign language education than any U.S. newsperson, with the exception of Fred Hechinger of the *New York Times.* In a series on foreign language teaching outside of the United States, she wrote this observation:

> In the United States, the general thought is that second (and third) languages are not taught very well, but that because so many people in Europe are multilingual, they must teach languages well there. . . . In fact, methods used to teach languages in the U.S. tend to be more intensive and thorough just because so few in that nation have an opportunity to hear a second language spoken fluently or to immerse themselves in a second culture.[10]

An immediate problem at all levels is the lack of nationally recognized proficiency tests for teachers and students. Perhaps between the Modern Language Association,

Middlebury College, and a few other resources, some widely accepted unified testing will evolve. At a minimum, tests should be agreed upon for high school teachers, for first-year high school students, for second-year high school students, for college teachers, for first-year college students, and for second-year college students. If existing tests need improvement, they should be improved. If not, steps should be taken to gain much wider recognition for them.

George S. Springsteen, director of the highly respected Foreign Service Institute of the Department of State, has suggested: "A strong governmental effort should be made to support development of a relatively simple (but reliable) system to test at all school levels in order to measure proficiency." [11]

Testing also tends to orient the teacher and class to specific goals. If the Spanish students at Blank High School took a nationwide Spanish test after their first year, the teacher, school administration, students, and parents would soon understand whether any real learning is taking place in their classroom.

Standardized testing for teachers and students is one step toward improvement in quality.

But what about the conscientious instructor who came into the ranks of teachers ill prepared, and who perhaps did not even realize it until recently? That teacher may fear any testing. If there is strong resistance from a faithful teacher, the administration could give that teacher a one-year notice, or even a two-year notice that testing will begin, to provide time for "brushing up."

Teacher competence is essential, but in itself it is not enough. Teachers use "tricks of the trade." The most successful somehow convey a sense of importance, a sense of vitality, a sense of fun at times. Successful teachers do not start out each session with an open-your-books-I've-got-to-go-through-this-routine attitude. The successful teacher has a sense of dedication, a sense of urgency. One of the most successful language teachers said: "If history has led anywhere, it is . . . that greater communication among peoples is necessary if we are to survive at all." [12] He believes that! Of the language teacher who has no sense of mission, he says, "If tenured, the uncommitted language teacher will dally for years in unpopulated classrooms."

I have collected a folder of notes about successful teachers I have seen in operation, and articles about successful teachers. Among the stories from my notes:

• St. Jerome believed that "sacred music is an essential element in Latin teaching." [13]

• Erasmus believed that conversations in the new language were much too dull, too polite for student interest. In 1524, he suggested there should be conversations like this:

> "Good day, you traveller's nightmare."
> "And good day to you, you glutton, epitome
> of greed, gobbler of good cooking."
> "My deepest respects, you enemy of all virtue."
> "Pleased to meet you, you shining example
> of unrightness."
> "Good morning, you fifteen-year-old hag."
> "Delighted, you eighty-year-old schoolgirl." [14]

• Virginia Bernardini of the Liceo Michelangiolo of Florence, Italy, teaches English and has the same students for five years, typical for Italy and many other countries. Her students score much above average in testing. Perhaps the key word is "involvement." She has students work in pairs on translations, has them study plays and poetry; they look at minority problems in the United States. Her courses are a study in British and American culture as well as the English language. She is in the middle of everything and has them in the middle of everything. When asked by a reporter if she expected other teachers to follow her methods, she replied with a laugh, "It's a dreadful lot of work, you know." [15]

• John Rassias of Dartmouth emotes. His classes are physical endurance contests for the teacher, sometimes for the students. He has been quoted as saying he will do anything to get his students interested. Well, almost anything. Mayhem is out, but pie-throwing is in. So is chair-breaking. National television and the news weeklies feature stories about Rassias. He has showmanship, but also substance. His students learn; they are enthusiastic. John Rassias does not do just what needs to be done to hold a job; his fertile mind is constantly thinking of new ways to stimulate student interest. The Rassias theory is that the teacher has to demonstrate by his or her energy and actions in class that he or she is genuinely concerned, that it is important that the student learn.

• Claire Gaudiani of Purdue University starts her French courses by asking each student to explain why they are in the course, what they hope to gain from it, and their strengths and weaknesses. She promises never to call on a student if his or her hand is not raised, but all must promise to volunteer answers at least once in each class session. Each student must preside over a seminar, in which the student lectures in simple French on a subject of choice, then moderates the discussion. She uses "study couples," combining weak with strong students. Students evaluate their own work regularly. One observer says she has "combined a spectrum of creative techniques with a little common sense and a great desire to trust, understand, and stimulate her students. To an overwhelming extent, they have justified her enthusiasm." [16]

• Bonnie Glyda teaches French at Eugene Borroughs Junior High School in Prince George's County, Maryland. In her classes there are "laughter, joking, sometimes a racket. Not a period goes by without fragments adapted from music-hall comedy, team cheers, television jingles, and even

Mother Goose. But the shenanigans are toward one end: the learning of French." [17] She stays in control of the situation, and says every class has a different personality, and adjustments must be made. A magazine writer noted: "What Glyda unmistakably communicates to parent and pupil alike is her enthusiasm for the French language." [18] She believes students should be exposed to foreign languages early in life and daily.

• Marta Bret teaches at the University of North Carolina at Charlotte. In addition to following textbook material, her students must write a weekly paragraph in Spanish about some topic related to the Hispanic culture: El Greco, the Moors, Jews in Spain, El Cid, etc. The students stand in front of the class, give their reports, and then answer questions and lead the discussion in Spanish. They learn songs and must sing them at the Christmas festival the foreign language department sponsors. She is interested and eager, alert to what is going on, and her students catch this.

It is clear that the finest of language lab equipment improperly directed will not produce a good language project. The teacher makes the difference. Some of the best teachers use the lab equipment—and some of the best teachers do not.

Today's textbooks are a vast improvement over those used in the days when I studied languages. In front of me, as I write this, is a German textbook that contains insights into German life and culture (as well as pictures) that make the textbooks of a few decades ago look dull indeed. All of the modern textbooks I have seen are substantially superior to their predecessors.

But I am convinced that the teachers I have cited as outstanding would be outstanding with old-fashioned textbooks.

In addition to an improvement in the tangible language tools, the second major factor in language technique that has emerged in recent years is the "immersion" experience. It has significantly improved the quality of language learning in the few schools using it. The Modern Language Association's Task Force on Institutional Language Policy states: "Despite ample evidence that students will become more competent faster in communicating in a foreign language by being immersed in the language and culture in which the language is used, distressingly few students have the opportunity for such language and culture immersion." [19]

Immersion at the elementary and secondary level means taking the regular curriculum in another language. In no way does it slow the student in any of the subjects covered. Costs are only slightly higher because textbooks must be purchased from France or Germany or some other country, though that would change rapidly if immersion started to grow in this nation. No additional teachers are employed, though securing those able to teach in another language may be a problem for a school board. It is much easier to work out an immersion program at the elementary level than at the high school level.

Immersion schools have until recently generally been private schools. One example is the Fleming School in New York City, a French-English bilingual school designed to teach French to children whose mother tongue is English. In Tegucigalpa, the capital of Honduras, there are four privately owned English-Spanish bilingual schools and one private French-Spanish school. Capital cities of most nations have such private schools.

Cincinnati, Ohio provides a public school example. When Cincinnati came under a court order to integrate students more fully, the school leaders decided, among other measures, to establish three schools, with different cultural orientations, one French, one Spanish, and one German. These elementary schools, which are roughly 50/50 black and white, have a long waiting list. I visited the schools and found them exciting. Imagine watching a fourth grade class in central Cincinnati, in an old school building, studying a biology lesson on the parts of a bird—in German! I understand why there's a waiting list to get into those schools. I wish my own children had had such an opportunity.

But should it take a court order on integration to get us to do something that makes so much sense anyway?

There are six small public school immersion programs in the United States. Immersion is fairly common, on the other hand, in Canada. One suburban Ottawa district has more elementary students in immersion classes than attend such classes in the entire United States. Of 2,100 students entering kindergarten each year in that district, one-third choose the French immersion program. Those entering span the full range in abilities and income background; it is not a program for the elite.

Immersion programs provide more time to absorb the language. Language scholar James J. Asher has noted:

> By the age of six a child has listened to his native language for 17,520 hours . . . based on eight hours a day for 365 days for six years. . . . In comparison, the student in the [traditional] classroom in one year has listened to a foreign language for 320 hours. . . . If we expect the student in the classroom to have the fluency of a six-year-old child, the student should listen to the foreign language for 55 years of college instruction. When foreign language is viewed from a time perspective, the mystery is that so much is accomplished in a highly condensed period of time.[20]

Immersion classes reduce that time differential.

Although Chicago, like every major city, has experienced the flight of people from the central city to the suburbs because of the condition of the schools, *Chicago Tribune* columnist Maggie Daly writes that

> a lot of parents with small children want to move into the Lincoln Park-Old Town Triangle neighborhood [because of] the new LaSalle Language Academy. . . . The Academy will

teach 450 children from kindergarten through 8th grade one or more foreign languages, including some Asian languages, in addition to full elementary education. It's part of the [Chicago Public Schools'] Board of Education Access to Excellence program. The children will use their foreign languages on field trips and in chatting with visitors to the school. The children, selected through a screening process . . . are an integrated cross-section of students.[21]

The public schools of Montgomery County, Maryland have "cluster schools" for French and Spanish. Here is a description of the "French Immersion and French Emphasis" school at a place called Four Corners:

Children enrolled in the French immersion classes learn their subject matter in French. An immersion class is like any other, except the children use French, rather than English. They are taught throughout the day in French, learning to speak, read, write, and think in that language, while mastering the basic skills in the elementary school curriculum. In addition to becoming fluent in French, students gain deeper insight into the culture.

Parents must apply for their children to enroll in the French immersion program and students with varying abilities are accepted. Those starting French immersion in fifth and sixth grades are admitted on an individual basis in consultation with the principal. Kindergarten children are not admitted to the program. Classes in French immersion are often groupings of three grade levels. All school-wide programs are an integral part of the school for all students. Parents are asked to support the program—showing their children they believe learning in French is important. Parents attend meetings, volunteer, take French classes, or show their support in various other ways. These parents meet regularly to discuss concerns and receive tips on how to help their children. The first few months in the immersion program can be difficult for some children, but using a foreign language all day becomes natural and comfortable once they begin to master enough French to function well. Those considering the immersion program should visit the school with their children and attend orientation sessions.[22]

The program started in the fall of 1974 with 20 students in grades one through three, and in the 1978–79 school year had 120 students in grades one through six.

Middlebury College in Vermont is the outstanding U.S. collegiate example of such a program, its summer immersion program attracting about 1,200 students from throughout the nation. At Middlebury, students pledge that for six to nine weeks they will not speak English. Middlebury offers a choice of seven languages. Its faculty is drawn from around the world. Cost for students is about $1,000 for six weeks, $1,400 for nine weeks.

John Rassias's physically active language immersion program (part of regular academic year courses at Dartmouth) is being adopted at other institutions. The University of North Carolina (Chapel Hill), William and Mary, the University of Detroit, Howard University, and some fifty-one other colleges, universities, and community colleges are using the Rassias approach. Many of these schools received support money from the Exxon Education Foundation under its Impact program in order to initiate this approach.

Using a modification of the complete immersion practice, Earlham College in Indiana provides language classes five days a week for three hours a day. Several other schools have similar programs, programs that fit into the curriculum more easily than total immersion.

Although immersion programs are difficult to work into standard curricula, their effectiveness is unquestioned. George Williams College in Illinois has a fairly typical program utilizing limited time span efforts. Upon arrival at a weekend camp, students sign a pledge "to speak only the Spanish language from the moment I place my signature on this statement until I return from the George Williams College Spanish Immersion Weekend." The menu, directions around the camp, songs to be sung, all are in Spanish.

An intensification period can be geared to the specific

needs of a group. A lengthy curriculum would not need to be devised to accommodate the needs of a group of pharmacists who desire to learn Spanish, for example.

Some forms of immersion are available below the college level. Summer language camps lasting one week or longer have retained a limited popularity. Weekend language camps for a variety of age groups are growing in popularity. The Center for Slavic and East European Studies of Ohio State University operates a successful weekend *Lager Druzhba* (Camp Friendship) where Ohio State and area high schools cooperate. Jefferson County, Colorado, public schools operate one of the more successful programs in the nation for their Russian students. Jefferson County, incidentally, enrolls more Russian students than the entire state of Ohio.[23]

A host of schools offer overseas immersion opportunities, though a word of caution is in order. The *Christian Science Monitor* commented:

> Too many schools, colleges and private organizations offer a pseudo-immersion in a second culture, often claiming the gaining of skills and understandings that only true immersion can bring. Since one type of program costs about the same as the other, let the wise student—and his parents—beware. Find out just how much opportunity there is going to be for the student to revert to English, to read English newspapers, to be taught by English-speaking instructors, and to travel superficially in and out of several cultures. If your goal is to become more fluent in a second language and to understand another culture in some depth, then choose wisely. And if your own school or college only offers a superficial program, join one that is more demanding and will teach you more, transferring your knowledge if not your credits.[24]

Perhaps the most unusual of the immersion programs is at Dartmouth, where, after taking a language in the Rassias method, about 40 percent decide to spend a quarter overseas. Students are sent in groups of twenty-five, each living with a family in a provincial city. Then comes the excitement: "the village drop." After being in France (for example) for nine weeks, each student is assigned a village and told to go there, with no money; not a franc. He or she must hitchhike to the town, and convey the need for help to townspeople. At the end of three days the student is to return with a report on the history and structure of that community. The response: "Villagers always respond with hospitality, delighted to show the American around. They have thrown parties for the students and given them gifts. The students return from the trips with a warmth for the French people that few tourists or traveling students share." [25]

The thorny college-level question of whether a foreign language should have primarily a literature emphasis relates to quality, for so long as there is a heavy, often archaic, literary emphasis in the foreign language program, conversational language will suffer.

A 1957 survey of 443 foreign language teachers in Illinois asked what college courses they found most useful and what courses least useful. Interestingly, 103 found their foreign language literature courses the most useful, and 144 found them the least useful.[26]

The former Director-General of UNESCO, René Maheu, has observed that the greatest disadvantage of universities is their resistance to innovation. And a Swedish educator has written, "The ability of universities to implement profound changes and renewal is intolerably weak." He had this observation about Swedish language training: "The language departments of universities have traditionally devoted themselves to the training of language specialists, highly qualified in literature. . . . But now a new demand is added: short and effective language courses in the fields of engineering, natural sciences, social sciences." [27] A consultant's report on a foreign language department of a U.S. university notes: "The faculty, the departmental chairman, and the Dean of

Arts and Sciences reflect an isolationist attitude toward out-reach activities, and curricular or instructional innovations." [28]

Where there has been a shift away from the literature emphasis—at Washington State University, for example—an increase in enrollment in literature classes has often occurred. Dartmouth, under the Rassias influence, has deemphasized literature in language courses. Students gained competence in languages, and therefore enrolled in advanced literature courses.

But when literature study is the major aim, the ability of the language courses to attract a multidisciplinary interest will lag.

To achieve a shift away from a heavy literature emphasis is not easy on many campuses. One college faculty member who has been in this battle talks about "the stranglehold that tenured literary Ph.D.'s now hold on the colleges. . . . The veto power that the literary Mafia holds over any college reform must be eliminated." [29]

That puts the issue in extreme terms. The meshing of literature, technical language, and conversational language should not be difficult if assurances can be given that no faculty member will lose either job or status because of the shift.

More than a century ago, Macaulay wrote:

> My way of learning a language is always to begin with the Bible, which I can read without a dictionary. After a few days passed in this way I am master of all the common particles, the common rules of syntax, and a pretty large vocabulary. Then I fall on some good classical work. [30]

But what Macaulay could do, every student cannot do. And what he sought from a foreign language is not what a chemical engineer may seek from a language course.

A respected foreign language teacher, who did not want to

be quoted directly, said the following changes would raise the
level of quality of foreign language education:

1. Emphasis on quality at the high school level.
2. All teachers to be employed at any level, required to
   spend at least one year abroad.
3. Teachers hired to be interviewed in the language in
   which they will teach.
4. More flexibility on the requirement for a Ph.D. for
   teaching at the collegiate level. Some who have no
   Ph.D. are excellent teachers, some who have the degree
   are not.
5. Foreign language instruction five days a week—no
   three-day or two-day-a-week classes.
6. Teachers willing to fail students who should fail.

The Lambert study looked at the international studies
programs, and it suggests that criteria for a faculty member in
this field should include at least three years of residence in
the geographical area of competence, including a visit not
more than five years ago; an ability in one of the languages of
the area; and formal training in the area.[31]

As we upgrade the abilities of personnel in the foreign
language field, the closely allied international studies areas
should also experience improvement. That aggravates the
problem of quantity. Fortunately, there is growing recognition of the existence of the quality problem. But passive
recognition by administrators and teachers must be con-
verted to programs of action.

· 8 ·

The Less Traditional Approaches

> It cannot be overlooked that a large (and growing) number of Americans receive training in language through study under non-academic auspices.
>
> Statement of the Modern Language Association and other groups, 1973 [1]

> Although he became widely known in intellectual circles of the United States and Europe, Berlitz and his instructional system were met with skepticism by academic traditionalists.
>
> "The Berlitz Story" [2]

When the widely respected book, *Twenty-Five Years of Language Teaching,* appeared in 1969, it did not mention the Berlitz schools and their approach to language teaching. But to a great extent the successful language teaching tool of immersion grew out of the Berlitz schools. *Total Immersion* is a trademarked phrase owned by Berlitz and its parent company, the Macmillan Corporation. In many large cities of the United States, there are more foreign language students in for-profit language schools like Berlitz than there are in the colleges and universities of that city. And in some cities, more students are enrolled in the private language schools than in the language courses of colleges, universities, and public schools combined.

This is less a tribute to the private schools than a commentary on the status of foreign language teaching in our more traditional educational facilities. It is also significant that so many Americans for one reason or another do turn to the nontraditional schools for help, often quick help.

The Berlitz story is an illustration of the old adage that adversity is sometimes a blessing in disguise.

Maximilian Berlitz came to the United States from Germany, and in 1878, started a language school in Providence, Rhode Island. French was the major language interest in Providence at that time. He advertised in *The New York Times* for a French teacher and received a beautifully written application in fluent French from Nicholas Joly. When Joly arrived in Providence, Berlitz discovered—to his horror—that he knew no English. Desperate and sick with influenza, he told Joly to try to teach by pointing to objects. Six weeks later, Berlitz went to his school expecting to find disaster. Instead, he discovered the teacher and students carrying on conversations in French, and enjoying it. Students were far ahead of where they would have been under his traditional methods—and they were speaking French with less of an American accent. Berlitz knew he had discovered something, though perhaps *discovered* is too strong a word, for here and there educators for centuries had been suggesting the deficiencies of traditional language teaching methods. In 1570, for example, one scholar wrote: "All languages, both learned and mother tongues, be gotten and gotten only, by imitation. For as ye use to heare, so ye learne to speake; if ye heare not others, ye speake not yourself."[3]

The principle of speaking only the language being taught has been used by the Berlitz schools to this day. Currently thirty-nine languages are taught in these schools. More than half of the 500 top corporations listed by *Fortune* magazine utilize the Berlitz schools, the tuition tax-deductible for corporations, though ordinarily not for individuals. Travelers and students who plan to attend foreign universities are also prime sources of Berlitz recruits. Students of their programs have included President and Mrs. Jimmy Carter, Czar Nicholas of Russia, Katharine Hepburn, Enrico Caruso, Nelson Rockefeller, and Great Britain's Princess Anne. Among their faculty members have been Leon Trotsky, Emile Zola, and James Joyce.

Berlitz now operates 200 schools in twenty-two countries. The average school has twenty classrooms. Some cities have more than one school: New York City has three, Tokyo seven, Paris ten, and Mexico City six. While most teaching is done in classes, they also offer individual instruction and a Total Immersion program in which a student is taught for nine hours a day for from two to six weeks. All for a price, and their programs are not inexpensive. A minimum course with forty-five hours of instruction in a class, with a maximum of four people, costs approximately $500. A one-on-one Total Immersion program costs approximately $900 for one week.

Berlitz finds some increase in demand for language teaching in the United States—but much greater demand in other countries. In 1968, lessons given in the United States accounted for 52 percent of the Berlitz world total. By 1977, that had slipped to 23 percent. Foreign utilization had risen from 48 percent to 77 percent. The two nations that show the greatest demand for the Berlitz courses are Japan and Germany.

One difference exists between Berlitz courses in the United States and abroad, a significant difference. In the United States, most language students are beginners, while in other countries 95 percent of those taking the courses already have a knowledge of the language but want to improve their fluency. This is despite the fact that most U.S. students are between the ages of thirty and fifty, while in other countries, Berlitz finds that most students are between twenty and thirty-five.

Raphael G. Alberola, the president of Berlitz, makes this observation: "We see at Berlitz case after case where students come to us reporting prior negative experiences [in foreign language study] and then go on to become enthusiastic students" [4] at Berlitz. There is probably some degree of institutional pride in that statement and a bit of self-promotion. But there is also much truth. Those involved in more traditional academic courses would do well to ask themselves the reason. Part of it is that when students come to Berlitz, they genuinely want to learn and want to learn enough to pay a substantial fee. Another reason may be that Berlitz does not need to worry about academic tenure. But a substantial part of it is method. Academics fool only themselves if they do not recognize that reality. Dr. James Conant had been one of the critics of the Berlitz approach, but when the president named him U.S. High Commissioner for Germany in 1953, he took a Berlitz course!

The president of Berlitz makes another insightful observation:

> It isn't easy to be a Berlitz school director. You have to have a fluent command of at least two languages. And very few Americans qualify, unfortunately. This isn't true in other countries. In France all but two of our directors are French. In Japan all but one are Japanese. In Spain all of them are Spanish. In Latin America all but one are Latins. In Germany all of them are Germans. But in the United States—where we operate 59 schools—there are only eleven American-born directors. [5]

All Berlitz teachers are required to have native fluency. Emphasis is on speaking, rather than on reading or writing. There is no formal grammar instruction. The aim is to get students not only to speak another language but to think in that other language as well.

Other private schools claim that they do a more effective job of teaching—sometimes at less cost—than does Berlitz.

While these claims may be correct, none of the other schools approaches Berlitz in size. This chapter makes no attempt to weigh the individual merits of the various private operations. Many academicians are critical of the Berlitz-type approach. One reporter for the *Chronicle of Higher Education* who signed up for the minimum Spanish course, and found it generally effective, offered these criticisms:

1. The class of four included different levels of ability and foreign language background.
2. During the fifteen-week period, the reporter had three different instructors.
3. There was a bit too much salesmanship to take extra courses.

But, on balance, the reporter found herself proceeding at "a much faster pace than I seem to remember in my college French classes."[6] After the fifteen-week course, she went to Mexico to interview leaders of a medical school for a story and managed to get by—not with ease—but she conducted successful interviews.

In 1973, the foreign language associations issued a paper entitled "A National Foreign Language Program for the 1970's." They made three points about the Berlitz-type programs: "First . . . they are meeting needs that academic programs have ignored; second, that Americans are willing to pay for language courses that are flexible enough to meet their specific needs; and third, that the academic profession can learn much from an examination of non-academic programs."[7]

The armed services have a substantial interest in language training. One month before the Japanese attack on Pearl Harbor the Army started a small Japanese language training program at Crissy Field in California. When hostilities broke out between the United States and Japan and Germany, it became painfully obvious that the traditional training periods and traditional methods for foreign languages would not meet this immediate national need. The small Army operation expanded and gradually grew into what is now the Defense Language Institute at Monterey, California, which serves all the military services.

At Monterey, more than thirty languages are taught intensively, students attending classes six hours a day for five days a week. Classes average eight to ten students. The length of the course varies from twenty-four to forty-seven weeks. The institute is the only place in the United States where certain languages are taught. In 1978, 3,747 students received training there, training universally acknowledged as superior, training designed to meet specific military needs.

The military also has what it calls "non-resident foreign language programs," outside of Monterey. These vary from limited but substantial courses taken by about 4,000 people to a brief introduction to a language given annually to more than 100,000 prior to overseas assignments.

The service academies also stress foreign language training. West Point requires it and the Air Force Academy and Annapolis encourage it. Languages offered at all three academies include Chinese, French, German, Russian, Spanish; and on a limited basis, Arabic (at West Point and the Air Force Academy), Japanese (Air Force Academy), and Portuguese (West Point). Unfortunately, language instruction at the academies is declining, as it is elsewhere in the nation.

Television and radio are an effective means of communicating a new language, but the media are not used as much as they might be. In pretelevision 1931, one alert linguist noted:

> Have not some few million people learned the grammar and vocabulary of Amos and Andy? If, for commercial purposes, a great network can be spread over the nation, is it not conceiv-

able that the great universities of this country may be hooked up in an educational network by means of which high school classes everywhere may learn French, German or Spanish given by a native speaking his own language.[8]

Since that time, public educational television has arrived, and a national educational radio network is operating. Both have been used to a limited extent for language study, the two most widely known programs being "Sesame Street," which has worked a little Spanish into its format, and "Que Pasa," with a more limited audience, which has done a superb job of teaching Spanish in a nonponderous way. Much more could be done, but these networks, like their commercial counterparts, tend to respond to demand, and they perceive that public demand is not high.

Also contributing to language learning, however, are the 270 commercial radio stations that broadcast in Spanish, 44 of them full-time Spanish stations, and the other stations with times slotted for sixty-three different languages, such as Lithuanian. Designed to appeal to ethnic minorities within the United States, they are also popular with students who want to hear the language spoken well.

Luis A. Garcia, who heads the Garcia Schools of Spanish in Houston, Texas, wrote to one of his former students, who became chairman of the board of the Columbia Broadcasting System, about the possibility of a language-teaching program on commercial radio. He received a reluctantly negative response: "It has been our experience that there are very few radio listeners who want to work very hard at their radio listening, and that seems to rule out a program of the type you suggest."[9]

Cable television is a relatively unexplored area of commercial television. Its audience is limited—sometimes extremely limited—but some of their programs attract a larger audience.

Gary Orfield, professor of political science at the University of Illinois, has suggested that since educational television comes on late in the morning and goes off early in the evening, it would be relatively easy to add a half hour of programing in the morning and evening in the principal non-English language of an area (usually Spanish), a means both of communicating with that population and of exposing the television audience to another language.

Unorthodox is probably not the precisely correct term to apply to the language methods of small advanced research centers operating overseas largely with U.S. financial backing, but they are different, and different in a good sense. Such centers operate in Turkey, Greece, Egypt, Italy, Hong Kong, India, Japan, Taiwan, and elsewhere. They all provide a superior educational opportunity, but also all share a weak financial base, made weaker in recent years by the gradual withdrawal of foundation funds, and by the reduction of university and federal support.

Some of the centers are language-training oriented, others are not.

The Tokyo-based Inter-University Center for Japanese Language Studies is one of the best of these programs. Administered by Stanford University, it has the backing of ten U.S. universities and of the University of British Columbia. Of the $600,000 annual budget, $44,000 comes from the universities, the balance from a variety of other sources, including $150,000 from the U.S. Department of Education.

Each of the thirty-five students admitted must have had two years of college Japanese. Graduates and undergraduates can be admitted, though most are graduate students. The program consists of ten months of intensive Japanese. A large majority of those who teach Japanese studies in U.S. universities have attended the Tokyo center; they form a knowledge pool and an "alumni association" network for ready exchange of information.

An unusual U.S. institution is the Monterey Institute of

International Studies. A small school with a language emphasis, it began in 1955 as a civilian counterpart to the military language training program in Monterey. The two institutions continue to work together closely.

A fully accredited college for juniors, seniors, and master's candidates, Monterey admits no beginning or second-year language students; it has 500 full-time students and 100 part-time. Of its graduates, 65 percent enter the field of business, 22 percent enter government careers. It follows only Georgetown University and the Fletcher School at Tufts University in the number of alumni entering the U.S. Foreign Service. In addition to master's degrees in area studies or language, it offers a certificate in translation and/or interpreting. Almost half the faculty are foreign-born. The primary emphasis is on acquiring knowledge while you acquire language skills. If you are a French-emphasis student planning to enter business, your accounting course is in French.

The Monterey Institute also has an intensive summer program similar to that of Middlebury College, and offers brief training courses for business executives and their families who are soon to be sent abroad.

In 1947, Secretary of State George Marshall signed papers formally establishing the Foreign Service Institute. An arm of the State Department, the institute places a major emphasis on language skill development, though that is not its only function. Approximately 7,500 of the 13,000 institute enrollees are involved in language programs.

Sixty percent of those trained by the Foreign Service Institute are State Department personnel and their families, the balance coming primarily from other government agencies. Half of the 13,000 enrolled each year in everything from a one-hour-a-day course to a full program are trained in the United States. The others are trained in overseas programs, the major ones in Japan, Taiwan, and Tunisia. I visited the facility at Tunis and was favorably impressed both by the quality of leadership and the skills being developed by the students.

The Foreign Service Institute offers full-time language training in some forty languages, with the minimum length for a full-time course twenty weeks. In addition to these full-time courses, three-hour-per-day classes are available for dependents, and a part-time early morning program is available from 7:30 A.M. to 8:40 A.M. in six different languages. Eighty percent attendance is required or the student is dropped. The institute has developed a series of language textbooks and recordings available to the public in an amazing array of languages—everything from Kituba to Luganda.

The work of the Foreign Service Institute mushroomed after 1955, when for the first time the State Department decided to undertake a survey of language skills in the Foreign Service. Then the question emerged: How do you actually determine what a person's language skills are? Tests were devised and a system of evaluation of reading and speaking skills was developed, personnel being graded from S-1 and R-1 (weak) to S-5 and R-5 (like a native). Those measurements are still used.

While the overall numbers trained at FSI are significant, the total trained in a language for more than six months from 1954 through 1978 is only 1,417. The largest numbers are not surprising: Arabic 165, Russian 147, Vietnamese 129, and Chinese 123. Considering that this covers a fifteen-year span, these numbers are hardly substantial.

The Foreign Service Institute is making a significant contribution, though by the standards of many nations we still lag far behind in our diplomatic service language skills, to our detriment. There still is some truth, unfortunately, to the comments of an Iowa political leader, John A. Kasson, who had been appointed our representative to Austria by President Rutherford B. Hayes. In 1881 he wrote:

... We have few [U.S. personnel] who are really masters of any other language than English. . . . As a rule such agents content themselves with mere routine, and for ordinary discourse depend upon some poorly paid interpreter of foreign origin, of whom the English language becomes in turn the victim. . . . The real interpreter of our interests becomes at last an irresponsible and partially educated foreigner. It is to be greatly desired that the United States should escape from this condition of inferiority.[10]

Within the category of unorthodox approaches to language learning are the methods of people who teach themselves, through records they buy, books they read, or some other self-help process. No one knows how many fall into this category. Some are deceived into quick-fix foreign language courses that promise to enable them to "speak German like a diplomat." But many benefit by the variety of programs available. And some learn without benefit of formal programs. The newspaper account of the death of Dr. Ernst Scharlemann, a Lutheran minister who died in Chattanooga, Tennessee at the age of ninety-one, mentions that he spoke fluent French and German and that at the age of seventy-three he taught himself Russian. How many people have enriched themselves—and their country—in that way no one knows. Cato, the great Roman soldier and statesman, learned Greek at the age of eighty.

St. Petersburg, Florida has perfected something that a number of communities around the nation have tried: a folk fair. Sponsored by the St. Petersburg International Folk Fair Society, the annual four-day event gives insight into the multiple backgrounds that make up that community, and an insight—however brief—into the language, dress, cooking, and other cultural habits of various nationalities and regions. The society publishes a booklet of approximately ninety pages, in itself a major cultural enrichment project. Schools are a special target of the folk fair but the entire community participates.

The ways in which we learn a language and gain insights into other cultures are clearly not limited to the traditional academic approach. The nontraditional approaches serve a national need and often serve to pioneer language learning. Academia has its rigidities that sometimes serve the comfort of its leaders more than the needs of its students. Nowhere is that more clearly demonstrated than in foreign languages.

· 9 ·

State Leadership

America's educators took very much to heart the isolationist dictates of the Founding Fathers. Schools were tools consciously and relentlessly employed to "Americanize" an immigrant population. For America's schools to "internationalize" a now overly parochial population flies in the face of two centuries of educational thinking and practice in the United States. Yet fly we must.

Rose L. Hayden [1]

We simply do not have adequate and comparable information about what's going on at the State level. . . . Information about State efforts is meager, scattered and rarely in a form which lends itself to beneficial comparisons among programs.

Charles B. Neff [2]

Education in the United States has traditionally been the responsibility of the states, with the authority to carry out education programs granted by the states to local school boards.

Some states are doing better than others, but no state is doing as well as it should in foreign language teaching. Perhaps in every state some area of leadership on foreign language education could be detected, though in several states it would take an extensive search to find that area of leadership.

States mandate the teaching of drivers' education or consumer education or the history of the state. The tradition that the federal government should not get involved in demanding specific courses in the curriculum has never meant that the states cannot decide the curriculum and structure the financing of schools.

When the choices of what to teach are handed to the states without guidelines and without any plea from the President or top national educational authorities or from Congress, the states have felt that (1) they are free to do what they want; (2) they are doing a reasonably good job; and (3) they assume there are no pressing, national needs. And the federal government has been silent on the foreign language need.

Among states providing above-average leadership in foreign language training are two that are not often considered bastions of progress: Indiana and North Carolina. Both have been blessed with a few key university leaders at the University of North Carolina and Indiana University who have provided academic leadership to their immediate campuses, and a substantial influence beyond the campus. The foundations, particularly the Ford Foundation, have also played a significant role in these states.

In Indiana in 1970, a group of colleges and universities formed a Consortium for International Programs. The Consortium was originally college-oriented, but it soon became apparent that it should encourage international orientation in the lower grades also. It did so shortly after the Indiana State Department of Public Instruction mandated a full year of non-Western studies for the seventh grade, a full year of West European and Latin American studies for the sixth grade, and a full year of Anglo-Canadian-American studies for the fifth grade. The consortium and the mandate meshed. Workshops and seminars were conducted for teachers. The programs have not remained strong, but they have had an impact nevertheless.

Indiana University has an honors program for high school students who are at least in their third year of French, German, or Spanish. In this two-month summer program outside the United States, students live with foreign families. It is highly competitive, with only thirty students picked for each program. Costs are $1,100 for Mexico and $1,750 for Europe, but financial aid is available for students who need it.

Indiana University also is the site of the Indiana Language Program, "a unique ten-year project designed to extend and improve foreign-language learning in the state of Indiana." [3] Part of the function of this project is to collect data on statewide enrollment and teacher workload, and to assess the Indiana program.

The state legislature created the position of Coordinator for School Foreign Languages for the state of Indiana. This post is filled by Lorraine A. Strasheim, who provides leadership not only in her state but nationally. Her duties include collecting data; disseminating information to the teachers of the state through newsletters, conferences, and workshops; and working with the Department of Public Instruction and the state's universities to promote, and serve as liaison for, foreign language interests.

The state language coordinator describes Indiana as typical of the status quo in the nation, "for it ranks neither in the highest nor the lowest quarter . . . among the fifty states in numbers enrolled." [4]

Indiana has a statistical base of information better than that of any other state. It knows, for example, that

• In grades nine through twelve, in 1968–69, Indiana had 13,923 French students; in 1977–78, when school enrollments were higher, there were fewer—10,755 French students. German also dropped over the decade; Spanish was moderately stable; Latin dropped more than 60 percent.

• In the 1972–73 school year, 49 percent of the French teachers were full-time; by 1976–77, only 38 percent; German, 58 percent in 1972 and 48 percent in 1976; Latin fell from 21 percent to 16 percent; and Spanish, only slighly, from 58 percent to 54 percent.

• The average class size for first-year French in Indiana is twenty, German, twenty, Latin, eighteen, Russian, fourteen, and Spanish, twenty-two. Classes generally decline in size after the first year.

• The rate of drop-off from first year to second year of language has grown. The drop-off rate (leaving the language after the first year) for French is 35 percent; German, 36 percent; Latin, 48 percent; and Spanish, 53 percent. Lorraine Strasheim suggests that this drop-off is caused by a proliferation of electives, by the generally accepted myth that languages can be easily and quickly learned, and by the weakening of college entrance requirements.

Indiana, with 22 percent of its high school students enrolled in foreign languages, is above average among the states, though not outstanding. But then no state is outstanding. Indiana is doing better than many would expect it to do. Its detailed knowledge of what is going on in that state will be useful if the time comes when the programs must enlarge—and inevitably that time will come. Indiana is better prepared than most states to move ahead. It has developed a base in public opinion and in the knowledge of its strengths and weaknesses.

In July 1975, the North Carolina State Board of Education adopted a resolution reaffirming

its belief in and commitment to a vigorous program of instruction which will prepare North Carolina's children for effective participation in the world community and its belief that educators must have experiences with peoples of other cultures who are representative of the world community. The board further urges the leadership at the State and local levels to pursue avenues for expanding this element of the public school program.[5]

Like Indiana, North Carolina's public school leadership has a commitment to making students sensitive to the international dimensions of life. In 1970, the North Carolina Department of Public Instruction recommended a new social studies curriculum for the elementary grades and high school with a heavy emphasis on international aspects: "No longer can we afford to ignore developments in Africa, Asia, and Latin America. It is of vital importance that we rid ourselves of the myths and misconceptions we as a people have traditionally held concerning those whose cultures differ from our own." [6]

And while the new social studies curriculum does not include a foreign language emphasis, there is a spillover, just as a good foreign language course is also a course in international awareness.

Even before North Carolina installed this new curriculum, it had sympathetic school leadership that leaned in that direction; it has unusually fine leadership at the University of North Carolina and at Duke University.

The public schools of Charlotte, for example, have not experienced the drop in foreign language enrollment that the rest of the nation has experienced. Part of the answer is Evelyn Vandiver, an energetic former language teacher who now administers the foreign language program for the Charlotte schools, and conveys to administrators, teachers, and parents the importance of the program. Another part of the answer is that business leaders recognize the need. Foreign-based industries, primarily German, have located in Charlotte. The practical use of German and other languages suddenly became much clearer to business and industrial leaders who want to please the industrial newcomers—and to do business with them.

Probably the most significant of all factors is Craig Phillips, the State Superintendent of Public Instruction. As one North Carolina observer told me, "The bottom line in North

Carolina is that Craig Phillips really believes in the international dimension of education and he works hard for it. He did that even when it was bad for him politically."[7] Others voiced the same opinion, using words like *enthusiasm* and *dedication* to describe Phillips's role.

When a group of Japanese and American educators and leaders decided to experiment with a cultural exchange program, North Carolina was selected for the Japan project, to many people's surprise.

Phillips has surrounded himself with people who had similar goals and dedication, particularly Betty Bullard, who headed the international education program, and Denny Wolfe, who spearheaded the foreign language effort. Wolfe's predecessor, Tora Ladu, also provided leadership.

What was happening in the schools tied in with the needs identified by the state's political and industrial leadership. Three governors—Robert Scott, James Hunt, and James Holtshouser—had recognized the importance of international trade to the future of North Carolina. They promoted it among state legislators and among business leaders. Governor Hunt called a statewide meeting at which he stressed the importance of foreign languages and international education for the proper climate for industry. The result has been more exports from North Carolina, more foreign investment—109 major industries—in North Carolina than in most states, and a surprisingly good climate for the type of program Craig Phillips is promoting in the schools. Though there has been relatively little direct promotion of foreign languages by industry, the school program reinforces the industrial program, and the industrial program reinforces the school program.

The North Carolina Department of Public Instruction issued a statement in 1979 on foreign language education that minces no words: "We are no longer justified in considering foreign language study a frill when we admit our dependence on other nations and rank ourselves among international leaders." [8] It calls for teaching foreign languages in the elementary schools and is forthright in saying it. School officials who face elections (just as all others who face elections) have a tendency to walk softly, to say the right thing but not too firmly. Craig Phillips is nontypical in this respect.

Indiana and North Carolina have not been the only states to provide leadership. In Illinois, Superintendent of Education Joseph Cronin appointed a committee to examine the foreign language field. Superintendent Wilson Riles has done the same in California.

The New York education leadership has consciously and systematically promoted an international dimension to education, or at least it has until recently. That interest appears to have diminished. Illustrative of that decline is the drop in foreign language enrollment at the State University of New York from 1975 to 1977, an 8.7 percent drop, and at the City University of New York for the same years, a 20.1 percent drop, caused in part by New York City's fiscal problems.

The Texas Education Agency has tried to make bilingual education precisely that, rather than a form of monolingual education. A 1973 survey of Texas students, from kindergarten through high school, found 247,000 with limited English-speaking ability—but who spoke among them fifty-one dialects and languages. Of that total, 240,000 spoke Spanish. Among the goals the Texas state agency has adopted for itself is the preservation and strengthening of the various languages spoken in Texas and the extension of "bilingualism through bilingual education for the native English speaker. . . ." [9] The State Board of Education approved a goal to "promote more and better instruction in modern foreign languages."

Louisiana has a state-supported organization called the Council for the Development of French in Louisiana. Founded and headed by a lawyer, James Donengeaux, its aim is to retain the French language ties of the Louisiana heritage. He comments, "I began with the recognition that cultural blindness and provincialism were contrary to the national interest and Louisiana's interests. We in Louisiana had a great natural advantage to learn two languages with equal facility, and that culture was being lost. Something had to be done."[10] The council secured "foreign aid," $3.5 million from France, Belgium, and Canada (the province of Quebec) which brings teachers from these countries—and French-speaking Tunisia—to Louisiana. For the 1979–80 school year, more than 300 visiting teachers are promoting French. The "foreign aid" is matched by $290,000 in state and federal funds.

Wisconsin has done an above-average job in promoting the general concept of international education. Hawaii, Nebraska, Iowa, Michigan, Rhode Island, Pennsylvania, Wyoming, and Ohio at one point or another have also made some above-average efforts.

Some encouraging things have happened in California. The state had passed a law mandating foreign language classes in all schools. No one enforced the law; in 1969, the legislature revoked a host of requirements then in effect for the curriculum, including the foreign language requirement.

The state has mandated by law that bilingual classes should be one-third composed of people whose native tongue is English, and two-thirds, non-English-speaking students. While that requirement technically violated the federal law until recently, it opened the door for language opportunity to many students.

The present emphasis in California is on bilingual education, with other foreign language study slipping, according to Davis Campbell, the Deputy Superintendent of Public Instruction in charge of programs. Campbell blames much of the slippage on the colleges and universities. "When they eliminated the foreign language requirement, the motivation disappeared for the high schools," he relates with a tone of regret.[11]

The state of California has issued two reports on *Foreign Language Framework for California Public Schools, Kindergarten through Grade Twelve*. In 1970, the California State Foreign Language Advisory Committee adopted a set of principles that includes:

• All California students should be given the opportunity to study foreign languages.

• The school curriculum in California should include foreign language instruction in kindergarten and grades one through twelve.

• A language is better understood, and learning is increased, when the cultural background of the people who speak that language is incorporated into an educational program.

• Students should be encouraged to begin foreign language study early in their academic careers.

• Instruction in foreign languages should be offered daily.

• School districts should offer more than one foreign language.

• Teachers and administrators should explore the use of paraprofessionals—both paid and volunteer—to increase the effectiveness of foreign language instruction.

On the negative side for California, the lack of requirements by colleges discourages foreign languages, and the passage of Proposition 13 has caused a cutback in "frills" at schools. Unfortunately, some school administrators and school boards regard foreign language teaching as a frill.

The Lambert study, referred to earlier in this volume, made a state-by-state analysis of placement of international area studies faculty. It listed the percentage of international studies faculty at the college levels in each state.[12] I had that datum interpreted in relation to the population of the state to get a relative idea of how the states are doing in numbers of faculty in international studies. For example, the Lambert study showed that Minnesota had 1.96 percent of the area studies faculty of the nation, but has slightly less than that in percentage of the national population; thus Minnesota has a ratio of 1.07 in this analysis. The table (below) has several weaknesses: It cannot measure quality; it does not

Faculty-Population Ratios
(based on Lambert study)

Washington, D.C.	5.25	Oregon	.66
Hawaii	3.29	Tennessee	.65
Connecticut	2.35	New Jersey	.62
Massachusetts	2.15	Kentucky	.61
Vermont	2.14	Virginia	.58
New Hampshire	1.69	Florida	.55
New York	1.59	New Mexico	.51
Wisconsin	1.55	Texas	.50
Indiana	1.54	Nebraska	.49
Colorado	1.52	Nevada	.48
Michigan	1.36	Maine	.48
Illinois	1.29	Wyoming	.47
Kansas	1.27	Louisiana	.44
Utah	1.15	Georgia	.43
California	1.10	West Virginia	.41
Arizona	1.09	Montana	.40
Rhode Island	1.09	South Carolina	.35
Minnesota	1.07	Idaho	.35
Washington	1.07	Oklahoma	.31
Pennsylvania	.95	Alabama	.22
Ohio	.94	Alaska	.21
North Carolina	.87	Mississippi	.13
Maryland	.80	South Dakota	.13
Missouri	.79	Arkansas	.07
Delaware	.78	North Dakota	.00
Iowa	.77		

directly relate to foreign language teaching; the Lambert study was published in 1973, and there have been changes since then, though few major ones. Nevertheless, the analysis does provide some insights into faculty-population ratio. Iowa stands at the midpoint among the states.

Some good things are happening in the states; this chapter has touched on only a few. It is nevertheless true that when we speak about state school leadership for foreign language education we are largely speaking about a vacuum. There is little hostility to such programs, but little leadership either. In some states, there are fine goals written on paper, but the performance differs substantially from the articulated goals. As a New York school official has noted: "We suffer from a rhetoric gap: what we say we do, or promise we will do, or exhort ourselves to do is often curiously out of phase with our actual efforts." [13]

· 10 ·

Jobs

Top management positions in many American corporations operating abroad are already held by foreign nationals, mainly because there are not enough American executives who speak the languages of the host countries. . . . The number of such positions [requiring foreign language skills] is on the increase, while the number of schools and colleges which offer the necessary preparation continues to shrink.

Fred M. Hechinger [1]

We have our own language barriers to break down. We need to fortify links with the administration, to learn how the academic enterprise looks from that particular point of view, and often to educate administrators in the realities of language education.

Quentin M. Hope [2]

There are three clear—but confusing—trends in the foreign language job market:

1. People with graduate language degrees—including Ph.D.'s—sometimes cannot find employment that utilizes their language skills in a meaningful way.

2. Employers may not be able to find the people with language skills to fill positions available.

3. Foreign language skills will become increasingly important in the employment market in the future.

These three realities are not as contradictory as they may appear.

Imagine that you apply for a job, and when they ask your

161

qualifications, you respond, "I speak English." It is unlikely that the employer will be impressed. The ability to speak English isn't enough. Nor is the ability to speak English and Spanish or another second language a guarantee of a job.

Language departments primarily train students to teach, but teaching jobs are scarce.

One disillusioned former language major with a bachelor's degree, who wrote to me, had become an ironworker, making more money than he would as a teacher, but unhappy both with his work and his original choice of college study: "All my years of language study would have been more profitably spent studying the use of office machines. . . . Today's students are wiser than I, hence they avoid the useless and take more vocationally-oriented subjects. . . . We must make the rewards of language study more practical, realistic and remunerative."[3]

Someone else wrote:

> Now in my third year of unemployment, I have sent out over 2,000 letters in quest of a position. I have five college diplomas, and am fluent in French and Spanish. My dossier is impeccable. Now at the absolute poverty level, I will have to turn to some dead-end minimum wage jobs, because there is nothing else open to me. Against me is the sin of being over fifty.[4]

In almost the same mail came a letter from someone complaining that he had to pay $12 an hour for French translating for his small business, and the translator had done a miserable job. Somehow we have to mesh those two needs, demand and supply.

Here is a letter from a Ph.D in Oriental Studies from the University of Pennsylvania:

> I am fluent in Chinese, with a basic knowledge of Japanese and Spanish. I can also read a little French. . . . . I have the best academic training, seven years' exposure to East Asian

life and society, and solid business experience. . . . However, after returning to the United States to establish my career . . . I find that much of America does not appreciate the value of solid knowledge of, and experience in, a foreign culture. This is especially surprising in the case of China considering our new and increased concerns there. In the last seven months since my return, there have been about six openings in academia for a Sinologist throughout our country. This reflects the lack of concern in our education system. My investigation of government service possibilities revealed a similar attitude. . . . In commerce, only those international corporations which have learned from hard experience the value of in-depth cultural and linguistic knowledge have been willing to sit down with me and explore the possibilities of linking my expertise with their operational concerns in East Asia.[5]

He enclosed an impressive résumé and pointed out that few who need his particular talents know of them, and that those who have the talents do not know where to go to find those with the needs. He adds. "I know personally of many young orientalists who have left the field out of sheer frustration in not being able to find suitable employment."[6]

When the Modern Language Association met in New York at the end of 1978, the *Washington Post* ran a Depression-like story. It described what it called a "dance of desperation" in which, every year, the MLA "sets up its giant employment machinery, a great system of interviews designed to bring job seekers together with college department heads. At the same time, it spreads the word that there are virtually no jobs available. Here, before your very eyes, a celebrated chronic condition springs to life: the Ph.D. job gap. For years, America's universities have been spewing them out, then refusing to take them back in. . . . 'In our standard form letter,' said Roy Chustek [of the MLA staff], 'we tell people you must expect 100, 200, 300 applicants for one job paying $11,000 or $12,000.' "[7] One small sentence buried in the story is significant. "For the first time, the association invited to its convention hirers who are not academic—people from business, publishing and journalism."

A foreign language magazine observed as early as 1974, that "the downward trend of the rate of academic employment for Ph.D.'s is noticeable." [8] One expert in the field suggests the possibility that "only ten percent of the new doctorates will find employment in academia in the 1980's." [9] At institutions like the Fletcher School at Tufts University, the School of International Affairs at Columbia University, and the School of Advanced International Studies at Johns Hopkins University, a substantial shift already has taken place, both in the goals of students entering, and in their placement. Many banking and business graduates are entering these three institutions.

Jung Tschen of Iowa City is a Chinese citizen but a permanent resident of the United States by choice because he is the father of a United States citizen. He told me in a letter that he speaks fluent Russian, Chinese, German, and English, but at age fifty-eight and without U.S. citizenship, he has had to struggle to get a job. He believes the United States needs language proficiency standards and that foreign citizens should not be excluded from employment. More and more U.S. corporations are following such a policy. Unable to get Americans with adequate language skills, they utilize foreign nationals. One advertisement extolling the virtues of glass, told the story of Owens-Illinois. It included these lines:

> As the world shrinks, O-I expands. With a new glass container plant in Puerto Rico and increased capacity at plants in Brazil and Venezuela. So we can better serve growing markets throughout Latin America. O-I has investments in 81 plants in 21 foreign countries. Remarkably, only 40 Americans are employed in our international work force of 32,000.

The advertisement did not say *why* so few Americans are employed abroad. Coca-Cola in Japan has refused "to hire any American for a management position."[10] An officer of another corporation has stated that "You can't bring Middle West language and customs to the Middle East and be a business success. If we have a choice of hiring an American executive who speaks only English or a national of comparable executive skills who speaks the local language plus English, the choice is not a difficult one."

The Joint Committee on Eastern Europe of the American Council of Learned Societies notes that unemployment is "particularly acute among East European specialists since their substantive and language courses tend to be eliminated in order to maintain Russian language instruction and courses on Russia and the Soviet Union." It points out that

> the national interest is not to be measured in employment figures, but in the availability of an adequate pool of top-level, thoroughly reliable East European specialists. . . . . Much of the concern about a possible oversupply of specialists is exaggerated and misdirected. Present numbers of qualified people are too small, rather than too large, for the requirements of government service, education and business in a first-class world power like the United States.[11]

The Association for Asian Studies says, "Unemployment of specialists in the Asian studies field is relatively low, but underemployment is increasing, as specialists take positions in which they make only limited use of Asian skills."[12]

A small paragraph in a story on the sports page of the *Washington Post* noted that baseball teams are increasingly employing Spanish-speaking managers while other managers—Earl Weaver of the Baltimore Orioles and Billy Martin then of the New York Yankees—are trying to learn enough Spanish so they can speak to their Hispanic ballplayers.[13]

Pope John Paul II made a triumphal tour of the United States, speaking in slow, measured English—one of seven languages he speaks, and he knows phrases and sentences in a dozen more. Some day there may be an opportunity to elect an American pope—but will he (or by then, she?) be eligible by the criterion of knowledge of languages for serious consideration?

Alice Kent Taub and Teresa H. Johnson of the department of foreign languages of St. Louis University accumulated classified ads, gathered mostly from the Sunday issues of *The New York Times* over a two-month period, from employers seeking people with language skills. They sent them to me. I counted 631 ads in *The New York Times* for positions from secretary to engineer to accountant to teacher. A sizable number of employers are seeking people with knowledge of foreign languages. Significantly, most required two skills: foreign language *and* engineering or whatever the field happened to be.

A 1974–75 survey of 6,000 business firms, with 23 percent responding, reported more than 60,000 jobs requiring a second language. Assuming that the remaining 77 percent of the firms would at least double that number, at least 120,000 jobs among major U.S. business firms require a foreign language.[14] Most estimates place that figure substantially higher.

In Chicago recently, I glanced at the yellow pages of the phone book under "translators and interpreters," a list of seventy-one companies, from AAA Languages Services, Inc. to Universal Languages-Irsa Enterprises Inc. Some of those listed clearly are substantial companies employing a considerable number of people in a variety of language fields.

The Red Book Hotel and Motel Guide now lists the foreign languages spoken by personnel of various U.S. hotels to help the foreign traveler. I asked the manager of a hotel that listed only one foreign language skill about that, and he responded, "I'd like to do better. We've lost some Japanese and French business that I know of, and who knows how much additional business. But it's hard to find hotel management people who know other languages."

Tourism is a growing business in the United States, yet we are inadequately prepared for it. *Time* reporter Jane O'Reilly accompanied a group of French tourists in the United States, and from the Grand Canyon area reported: "At the El Tovar Hotel, a 1905 rustic masterpiece, members of the group wander through the corridors, searching for their rooms—yet another hotel without a French-speaking person on the staff. Although 20% of the visitors are now foreign, Amfac Inc., which runs the Grand Canyon National Park Lodges, has put up only some signs in Japanese." [15] The better hotels increasingly will be offering fuller language services, just as will the other arms of tourism, such as restaurants. Miami, through the accident of political events ninety miles away, experienced an influx of Cubans. Attuned to the Spanish-speaking customer, it has become a mecca for Latin American tourists. The Miami experience is not going to be ignored by businesses in other cities, who will be seeking clerks and managers, nurses and accountants who can speak another language. In Miami, it is easier to get a job almost anywhere if you can speak both English and Spanish. It is not uncommon for employers to hire someone who speaks only English on the condition that he or she study Spanish. The Greater Miami Chamber of Commerce has gone on record in favor of more language training "for job skills." And the language demands in Florida are broader than the tourist-related industries. Driving near Tarpon Springs, Florida, my wife and I saw a large sign for St. Petersburg Junior College, advertising a course that was about to begin in "Real Estate Spanish."

In theory, the number of teaching positions in the foreign language field should decline. That is based on the combination of the already declining enrollment figures in foreign languages, and the reduced enrollment in our schools we will be experiencing for the next decade. But that theory may run into a major obstacle that I hope this book will help to erect:

the reality that this nation has to do something to reverse present foreign language trends. And while we seem to be slow in learning that lesson, that reality is going to descend on us. Foreign language instructors may be in greater demand than others during the coming decade. That will be particularly true where teachers can accommodate themselves to the multidisciplinary approach, such as the "Joint Venture Program" of Appalachian State University in North Carolina, where students major in international business *and* foreign language.

Pennsylvania has compiled a detailed analysis of employment of those receiving baccalaureate and higher degrees in all fields, foreign languages among them. Their findings: [16]

• While 12.8 percent of those receiving baccalaureate degrees are unemployed, 14 percent of the graduates with foreign language majors are unemployed.

• The situation improved in 1978 over 1977, more than in any field except the study of law.

• Those planning to be foreign language teachers have among the lowest rate of placement in their chosen profession. That percentage was low in 1977 (41.6 percent) and lower in 1978 (40.9 percent). Most foreign language majors are employed in other fields.

• Five and a half percent of those receiving master's degrees in Pennsylvania in 1978 are unemployed, while only 3.6 percent of those receiving master's degrees in foreign languages are unemployed.

• Four percent of those receiving doctorates in Pennsylvania in 1978 are unemployed, but none receiving doctorates in foreign languages are unemployed.

• Of those receiving bachelor's and master's degrees in foreign languages, those specializing in French had the most difficult time securing positions.

The teacher-training emphasis of foreign language departments must change. One observer of the teacher position hunt has commented, "Many of those language arts concentrators now in the academic job market are applying for positions they have no real interest in, at institutions they do not really want to move to and which demand special qualifications they do not possess."[17] The author, a Ph.D. in German who works for the International Division of the National Savings and Loan League, makes this significant observation:

> Unlike our colleagues in the physical and social sciences, any Ph.D. in . . . German literature, say, who holds a full-time job anywhere outside a university or college is commonly said to have "left the field." The idea that a serious scholar might *choose* to support himself at some occupation other than teaching has been so completely ignored that leaving the university is tantamount to banishment in the minds of many students and professors. As a result, students with even a slight degree of interest in foreign languages or literary analysis often struggle along through graduate school and confine their job-seeking attempts to the teaching profession, even though they lack the ability to perform outstandingly as teachers or scholars.

Obviously the aim of this book is not to discourage people from entering the teaching profession, but we have ignored so many other options. The evidence of the internationalization of our society and of the job market is everywhere. Recently, when I got into a taxi at Kennedy Airport in New York City, the cab dispatcher handed me a slip of paper in five languages, explaining the cab fare system. If you get off a bus at the Port Authority terminal in New York City, there are now thirty-four young men and women in red blazers and navy blue slacks to assist you, one-third of them required to speak either Spanish or French.

Perhaps there is no institution as solidly imprinted with the "U.S.A." label as Sears Roebuck and Company. They now have a Spanish edition of their catalog, and the officers of the company proudly point out that that is not a new tradition. In the first catalog, which came out in 1888, Richard Sears, the founder of the company, wrote: "Tell us what you want in your own way, written in any language, no matter whether good or bad writing, and the goods will be promptly sent to you." [18] Ordering instructions in that first catalog were also written in German and Swedish to accommodate the immigrant population.

Ross R. Millhiser, number two executive in the $5-billion-a-year Philip Morris Inc., is quoted by the *Richmond Times-Dispatch* as stressing the importance of foreign language to business in the future. "Those who speak only one language will be at a disadvantage," he states, and described our inability to speak other languages as "one of the chronic deficiencies that plagues Americans." [19]

Howard Van Zandt is professor emeritus of the University of Texas at Dallas. At the age of ten, he moved with his family to Japan for five years, and he learned Japanese. He followed through on his Japanese, equipping himself with fluency in both Japanese and French. Listen to his story:

> During the Allied Occupation of Japan I served as a civilian telephone engineer on MacArthur's staff, and my Japanese language was of much value. There were many times when I was the only person who could communicate in both languages.... From 1956 to 1972 I was in charge of the interests of the International Telephone and Telegraph Corporation in Japan and some other Far Eastern countries. I served on 18 boards of directors, including those of two of Japan's great manufacturing companies. I could serve on boards because I could communicate in the language of the Japanese directors. When President of the American Chamber of Commerce in Japan, in meeting with Nippon groups, I gave my speeches in both Japanese and English. Between 1956 and 1972 I was interviewed on nation-wide television—in Japanese—twelve times.... Such success as I had overseas was due in large measure to the fact that I could speak the

language of the country in which I lived, and [could] understand the culture of the people. You may understand my amazement on returning to the U.S. to live to find professors declaring that it was unnecessary to require study of foreign languages or foreign cultures by students in courses in international management! [20]

Columnist Sylvia Porter had this advice on careers:

Teaching, law and veterinary medicine once were considered sure and safe careers. But all three fields are overcrowded today—telegraphing the disturbing message if you train for a job which looks great in 1979, how can you be certain it will even be in existence 20, or even 10, years from now? The answer: You can't be certain. But whether you are a young student selecting your college major, a parent trying to guide your children, or one of the growing numbers of adults seeking a second career, there is one move you can make as a form of "insurance" for just about any career. Learn a foreign language. [21]

An officer of Pan American World Airways, complaining about the steadily diminishing availability of language skills in our country, pointed out that their flight attendants must have conversational and reading skills in another language.

For the last two years our flight service recruiting team has experienced unprecedented difficulties as a result of the majority of the applicants' inability to meet the language requirement. . . . . In order to fill 40 flight attendant positions in 1977 our recruiting team had to interview 16,000 applicants! Almost 70% of the rejection ratio was due to insufficient language skills. [22]

The Ford Foundation has strong language requirements for its overseas staff—much stronger requirements than does the United States government.

How important is language skill to someone whose job takes him abroad? A vice-president of Chase Manhattan

Bank, upon returning from Argentina, said that going to another country without language training "is kind of like being a banker without accounting." [23] The *Wall Street Journal* carried this item:

> When a big Midwestern manufacturer bought into a Brazilian company early this year, it hastily dispatched three of its top technicians to shore up the sluggish Latin outfit. The American concern was in such a hurry that it didn't even teach its men or their families Portuguese, the language of Brazil. The results were disastrous. The American experts couldn't communicate with the Brazilian workers, and production started falling off. Their families, isolated by the language barrier and new culture, couldn't adjust; two of the marriages started falling apart, and the husbands put in for transfers back to the U.S. After six months, the company concluded that the two "just couldn't operate" in Brazil, and they're now heading back home. The third family belatedly is enrolled in Portuguese classes. [24]

Because our standards for translators and interpreters are almost nonexistent—anyone can advertise himself or herself in a telephone book as a translator or interpreter—the results are often less than completely satisfactory. But a person or firm maintaining high quality can on occasion draw substantial fees. Agnew Techn-Tran charged Hughes Aircraft $375,000 to translate technical documents of nearly two million words, according to the *Wall Street Journal.* That obviously is not typical. Many excellent translators struggle to exist, living in a world that is either "feast or famine." But the opportunities will grow. Plenum Publishing Company of New York and Washington recently signed an agreement to publish some Soviet technical works in English, an agreement that the president of the firm said could mean $87 million in U.S. sales and $8 million in royalties for the Soviets. It will also mean some jobs for top-quality translators.

At the United Nations, 110 simultaneous interpreters

work, each required to know thoroughly two other languages in addition to their mother tongue. Because simultaneous translation is a physically draining experience that requires constantly alert performance, these people work a maximum of twenty-one hours a week. The head of the interpreting program at the UN, George Klebnikov, comments: "An interpreter must remain as lively as possible. Some of the best young interpreters are trained actors. If a delegate tries to be funny he wants to be able to see that people who don't understand his language are also laughing."[25] The United Nations in 1976 published a sixteen-page document outlining legal protections they recommend for translators, and some steps nations can take to upgrade the status and improve the quality of translators and interpreters, another indication of their growing importance.

An often overlooked area for using foreign language skills is the labor union field. Many of the unions must work with ethnic minorities and some have foreign language publications.

Two publications that might be helpful to someone seeking a job are *Career Opportunities in the International Field,* published in 1977 by Georgetown University's School of Foreign Service, and *The Overseas List,* published by Augsburg Publishing House of Minneapolis in 1979.

A few other facts suggest where we may be heading:

• An increasing percentage of the top corporate officers of the nation have had some overseas experience and speak another language.

• Corporate officers who have been overseas agree that a "working knowledge of a foreign language" is "very important" for anyone who is to represent their businesses overseas.[26]

• Business views the hiring of Peace Corps alumni favorably because they understand both a foreign language and a foreign culture.

One of the problems on many campuses is inadequate job counseling for foreign language students. The language departments have not prepared themselves for it. This is gradually changing, and will change more. As the faculties of foreign language departments look at the job market outside of academia more seriously, there will also be an improvement in curriculum because the process of looking at job opportunities will sensitize them to the needs of the nonacademic world.

Just as language departments must be more aggressive in placing students and reaching beyond the academic arena, so they must also be more aggressive within academia. The sense of vitality and importance the faculty must convey to students must also be conveyed to administrators. Supine language departments are going to be run over.

The job situation is not rosy, but not as bad as is often portrayed. And it will get better inevitably, much better—if.

The big *if* is if language students, language faculties, and administrators recognize the areas of demand. It is not only in their interest that they do so, it is in the national interest.

· 11 ·

A Commission—and Hope

I fully expect that the Commission's report later this
year will give us all a greater appreciation of the value of
language study and of the role of language teachers in
helping us to fulfill our global obligations. . . .

Jimmy Carter [1]

Commissions tend to produce sweeping, noble statements
while ignoring the grubby details that might breathe life into
those pronouncements. Many impressive reports do nothing
more than gather dust. But there is reason to hope that the
Commission on Foreign Language and International Studies,
created by President Carter in April 1978, will generate action.

I had been concerned for some time about our language
deficiencies and the insensitivities to other cultures that have
resulted from it. Like many others who have been concerned,
I had offered no remedy; but then, after the signing of the
1975 Helsinki Agreement among thirty-five nations at the
Conference on Security and Cooperation in Europe, Congress passed a bill creating a watchdog committee. I was one
of six House members. The others were four presidential
appointees and six members of the Senate. I read the lengthy
Helsinki document and was pleasantly startled to read that
the United States had agreed to promote the teaching of
foreign languages and the understanding of other cultures. I
read a *New York Times* article by Fred Starr, Soviet scholar at
the Smithsonian, about our national language deficiencies,

and telephoned Starr to verify some facts for a weekly column I write for the newspapers and radio stations in my Illinois district.

Starr and I met for breakfast to discuss what could be done to meet our obligations. He suggested, as a start, a presidential commission; for such a commission to succeed, he said, it must have the imprimatur of the President. It occurred to me that the Helsinki oversight committee might be the appropriate place to begin. When several of the members agreed, I prepared a request to the President from the Helsinki Commission. The request was unanimously approved, thanks particularly to help from Rep. Dante Fascell of Florida, Rep. Millicent Fenwick of New Jersey, and Sen. Claiborne Pell of Rhode Island. I discussed the matter with President Carter and others at the White House. They agreed to create the commission. The President asked U.S. Commissioner of Education Ernest Boyer and me to put together a rough-draft list of personnel. What emerged was somewhat different from our list, but a substantial group. The President named James Perkins, former president of Cornell University, as chairman of the commission.[2]

I have served on many boards, committees, and commissions, but never on one where the attendance was as high and members more conscientious. Barbara B. Burn, director of the international programs at the University of Massachusetts at Amherst, headed the staff; her two chief assistants were Nan Bell and George Vaught.

I had two fears: first, that the interests of elementary and secondary schools would be ignored; and second, that the dominance of academicians would make decision-making difficult. I have learned that many in the academic community enjoy discussing decision-making more than making decisions!

My first fear was offset by others of the commissioners, including academicians. The recommendations for grade schools and high schools were, in the end, stronger than I suspected they might be. My concern about decision-making was, despite some postponement of decisions, reduced by the essential practicality of the members.

The commission issued its report in October 1979. It had rendered an important service to the nation even before that. Its very existence, and the hearings it held around the nation, stirred interest and hope among language professionals who had been discouraged and pessimistic. Wherever hearings were held, more people showed up than had been anticipated. Articles about the problem appeared in newspapers and magazines.

What did the commission call for?[3] Its report, edited by one of the members of the commission, Fred Hechinger, included these recommendations:

• Regional centers to be established around the nation on college campuses to promote and coordinate foreign language teaching and international studies.

• Per capita grants to schools at all levels to be dispersed to encourage foreign language teaching. The grants would be modest—$20 to $55 per student—but would provide a message of federal concern and incentive for schools to strengthen their present programs, or introduce programs if they have none.

• A solid program of research into foreign language teaching methods to be supported in each state department of education.

• Assignment of a designated individual in each state with clear responsibility for foreign language and international studies. Each state should appoint an advisory council similar to those established in California and Illinois.

• The federal government to move more vigorously to fill positions that require foreign languages with persons who have the ability to speak them.

• Model school programs in international education to be

established, with federal assistance, in six unspecified states as demonstration to the nation.

- Better utilization of existing resources: ethnic and linguistic minorities, returned Peace Corps volunteers, American professionals who have spent time abroad, foreign students, and foreign visitors.
- Promotion of exchanges of persons between countries.
- Support for strengthening of library collections.
- Encouragement of nontraditional citizen education efforts.
- Centralization of college and university administrative efforts so as to provide multidisciplinary approaches.

Initial reactions to the report were largely predictable: The President, at first, could not find time to meet with the commission he had appointed to discuss the results—not an unusual phenomenon for a presidential commission in any administration. Stuart Eizenstat, who oversees domestic policy decisions at the White House, did meet with the commission twice and showed considerable interest; on Capitol Hill, although most members of the House and Senate yawned, members of the committee with oversight responsibilities for the Helsinki Accord had high praise for the report.

Its ultimate impact will not be clear for several years as its recommendations are analyzed, refined, debated, and—I hope—confronted.

· 12 ·

Follow-Through

We must either actively promote our participation in the growing world intellectual culture or we will become increasingly irrelevant to it.

Richard D. Lambert[1]

We have the responsibility to design a system of incentives that leads adequate numbers of individuals to make the choice [to study foreign languages] for themselves. The irony is that we have the means for training them at hand, a truly colossal accumulation of resources that have been developed to perform just this task for us. What is the incremental educational, public relations, or other input needed to persuade people to make use of them?

Edward Keenan[2]

Everything I have written up to this point will be meaningless unless there is, in baseball terms, a follow-through.

Let me be candid: Most of those who are interested in this subject are not accustomed to influencing public policy. That is part of the reason we are where we are. That must change.

What we need is a series of small victories. These are achievable. A relatively small number of people working for modest successes can turn things around. These are steps that should be taken now.

College and University Administrators

1. No student should be admitted to a college or university without some exposure to foreign language study. None should be able to graduate without it.

2. The multidisciplinary approach that includes foreign languages should be pushed. Each college should examine its own program to see if it is meeting today's and tomorrow's needs, or if it is still focused on yesterday's needs. Literature should be part of the foreign language curriculum, but should not dominate it.

3. No student should receive a degree in foreign language without either substantive overseas learning experience or intensive language exposure like that which Middlebury offers. I do not suggest these as substitutes for present programs, but as additions to them. If these programs cannot be worked out at a particular college or university, then that institution should cooperate with another to provide them.

4. More than the somewhat traditional two years of language study should be encouraged. The rewards—economic and cultural—increase with more than two years of study.

5. As foreign language teachers are employed—and they should be employed with more care—there should be an understanding that periodic foreign travel in a country using the language is expected. The school will need to help finance this program.

6. Testing of foreign language students should become automatic, at least after the first and second years of studies.

7. Language programs should be available near or on the campuses of the professional schools; students who might take a foreign language course will otherwise be discouraged by inconvenience.

8. A small loan fund should be set up from the endowment to lend funds to students and faculty who wish to travel outside the country. Some interest could be charged. My guess is that those who take advantage of it will later donate much more than the interest to the fund.

9. A college's international emphasis should be broad enough so that it is not solely Western European.

10. Colleges and universities should assist in the upgrad-

ing of language skills for high school and elementary teachers in the area.

11. One or two universities should sponsor meetings—and receive federal financial support—for the scattered innovative elementary programs around the nation. A Cincinnati teacher writes:

> Those of us who are involved with innovative foreign language programs in the elementary school need to meet and talk with one another. . . . We are not many in number; we are spread nation-wide; most us work in schools with limited financial resources. . . . . Not only can we provide valuable insights for one another, we can also serve as a resource to those schools and districts which would like to initiate a foreign language program. . . .[3]

12. The chancellor of the University of Houston has made an interesting suggestion: Since the bachelor of science degree originally meant that the graduate had no knowledge of Latin, not that he or she had a knowledge of science, the distinction between the two degrees today (virtually nonexistent in most schools) should be revived, with the bachelor of arts degree awarded to graduates with a knowledge of another language, the bachelor of science degree to those without it.

13. Schools able to do so should provide some form of scholarship incentive to language students, particularly to those who learn less commonly taught languages.

14. Just as publishing is formally or informally recognized in the academic institution, so overseas experience can and should be recognized in some way as an enriching experience for teachers.

15. Criteria established for selecting college and university presidents, should include some foreign language background and a commitment to, and an openness to, the international arena.

Teachers

1. Teachers should speak up. No one will believe a language is important if a teacher doesn't. School administrators, school board members, PTA officers, the college faculty senate, business and labor leaders should be told if deficiencies exist. It is more useful to come up with constructive alternatives than to be simply negative.

2. An immersion week, weekend, or set period of time should be proposed.

3. Faculty should take advantage of immersion language opportunities, either in the United States, or through a planned program abroad. And this should be planned *now.* "Some day" never comes. Expenses may be income tax deductions.

4. Teachers who have ideas should offer them. Gary Rundquist, who teaches at a community college, the College of DuPage, in Illinois, suggested the college offer a course in Norwegian; college administrators were doubtful, but at Rundquist's urging, officials agreed to list it among the courses offered. Eighty-nine people signed up.

5. Would a community support a language-emphasis grade school, or, in a large urban center, a language-emphasis high school? If the answer to either is in the affirmative, teachers should discuss the possibility with persons who share their interests, and consider how to pursue it.

6. If ethnic groups live in your area, representatives of their community should be asked to visit classes. It will whet the appetite of students to learn.

7. Teachers should avoid isolating themselves from other teachers and disciplines, or from the business community, which may support a stronger language program.

8. A language course for older citizens might be successful.

9. Some form of special recognition or award should be offered by the school or perhaps by a local Rotary, Lions,

Kiwanis, or Business and Professional Women's Club, or Chamber of Commerce to the outstanding student in each language. Other forms of recognition can and should be provided.

10. College and high school teachers should lead in volunteering to teach on a limited basis in the elementary schools.

Students

1. If a high school, college, or university does not offer the language a student wants to study, the student should talk to someone in the administration or on the faculty or board about it. School administrations respond to demand.

2. Students should talk to foreign language teachers about the possibility of a language (immersion) weekend.

3. College students who can afford it should consider spending one summer at a school with an intensive language program, or one year studying overseas, or both.

4. Students should develop both reading and conversational opportunities in languages they are studying. The goal should be fluency, not just an acquaintance with the language.

5. If a school offers only two years of a foreign language, a student should talk to a teacher, administrator, or school board member about adding a year or two. This should be done even if the class size is small; it adds academic excellence to the school.

At the Local Level (Elementary and Secondary Schools)

1. Any high school that does not now offer foreign languages should do so. If there is a local problem of financing, two school districts might combine efforts.

2. Where there is inadequate demand for a full-time teacher either because of low enrollment in the school or interest in a particular language (Russian, for example), the shared teacher will generally be a more effective solution than the part-time teacher.

3. When foreign language teachers are hired, schools should make certain that:

a. The teacher is interviewed by a person competent in the language to be taught.

b. The teacher has had some experience in a country that speaks the language to be taught.

c. The teacher understands that travel experience in that country should be renewed at least once every ten years. The school might assist this process by setting aside an additional $25 a month for each foreign language teacher with the understanding that the teacher may draw on that fund for foreign travel.

4. Periodic tests should be given to evaluate both the teacher's competence and to determine the students' level of achievement.

5. More than two years of a foreign language should be offered. To do less is to impose the pain of language study and withhold much of the reward.

6. As interest in foreign languages increases, our schools should, as those of most other countries do, require two or more years of a foreign language unless a student is excused.

7. A language-emphasis grade school, and, in a large urban area, a high school could be set up. At the elementary level, such schools are popular, and they cost only the expense of textbooks.

8. For black and minority students, who are particularly likely to be deprived of an opportunity for foreign language instruction, adequate opportunities must be provided.

9. Nonforeign language teachers should be encouraged to take foreign language courses. Albert Shanker, president of the American Federation of Teachers, speaks directly to this need.[4]

10. In bilingual education, the teacher should be bilingual; the student should be taught English while at the same time encouraging him or her to retain the original culture and

language; and students whose mother tongue is English should also participate in such classrooms so that students of both cultural backgrounds will learn more rapidly.

11. School administrators and school boards should make it clear that when a teacher is employed in any area—art, history, music, or any other—the school prefers a teacher who has some foreign language background. Multidimensional teachers are almost always better than those with a more narrow focus.

12. All counselors must know that it is school policy to encourage foreign language study. If counselors have had no foreign study, they should take such courses. Counselors should also be familiar with student exchange programs.

13. An all-expenses-paid one-week course at a foreign language camp might be awarded by school districts to the outstanding language student in each class.

14. Some communities should establish ties to another country whose language and culture is taught in the elementary and high school system.

At the State Level

1. The governor should send a letter to every school board member and/or state administrator stressing the importance of foreign language teaching to the nation and to the future economic well-being of the state.

2. State legislators and/or education committees in the legislature should survey the colleges and universities and state offices of education to determine the strengths and weaknesses of foreign language programs and leadership.

3. The governor should call a statewide meeting of representatives of companies that export or have the potential to export, foreign language teachers, and representatives of the chambers of commerce and labor unions. The meeting should stress the importance of exports ($1 billion in exports means 30,000 jobs) and foreign investment to the state.

4. Financial encouragement should be given to school districts that institute language-emphasis grade schools or high schools.

5. A mailing should go to all school counselors stressing the increasing job value of foreign language skills.

6. The State Department of Education and the State Department of Commerce should work together on the foreign language problem.

7. Programs should be designed to encourage foreign language study and exposure by groups now statistically low in such study, i.e., the faculties of community colleges and professional schools.

At the Federal Level

1. Aid can be provided partially to compensate elementary, high school, and college administrations for foreign language efforts.

2. Exchange programs can be encouraged, for both faculty and students.

3. International studies programs must be supported, including community efforts; but these programs need to be carefully planned to respond to national needs.

4. The Department of Education should prepare foreign language programs for cable and public television and commercial stations that may wish to use them (with some encouragement from the Federal Communications Commission). Many stations could use a half-hour program and go on the air thirty minutes earlier (or later) with little additional cost. Similar programs should be developed for radio.

5. Summer institutes or seminars should be provided for foreign language teachers, and for teachers in other fields. The federal government sponsored these for several years; they were strikingly successful.

6. "Demonstration programs" should be encouraged. For example, a demonstration program that requires that at one

U.S. embassy all personnel in the embassy must be able to speak the language of the host country, from the ambassador to the secretary to the Marine guards!

7. Positions designated as requiring foreign language competency should be filled by language-competent persons. More jobs should be so designated. For example, only twenty-six federal positions are now designated as requiring Mandarin Chinese. For the most powerful nation on earth virtually to ignore the language spoken by more people on the face of the earth than any other, simply defies belief.

8. Americans stationed overseas with the armed forces should receive a lump sum payment (say, $300) if they pass a minimum language competency test in the language of the host country, and permission to extend their stay in that country, actually a money-saver for the service budget.

9. Literature should be prepared for students on such questions as "What Foreign Language Should You Choose?" It should contain simple, practical guidelines for students interested in a foreign language but unable to decide which to choose. Another leaflet should be prepared for school boards and school administrators, explaining why it is important to the nation and to the students that foreign languages be offered by local schools.

10. Federal manpower programs, such as CETA, could utilize some of the people in the foreign-language community in teaching jobs.

11. A one-day national meeting jointly sponsored by the U.S. Departments of Commerce and Education should bring business and education leaders together to discuss their mutual language problems. Such a meeting should involve the "movers and shakers," the people who have the authority to act and know how to act.

12. Through establishment of standardized language tests of both teachers and students, employers can determine the adequacy of the language skills of a potential employee.

13. The level of library support for foreign language courses, both at the precollegiate or collegiate level, should be evaluated by the Department of Education.

14. The Department of Commerce should, in cooperation with the Department of Education, track down linguists and match them with the needs of the corporate community. This information, placed in a computer, could produce for a Chinese expert seeking a job, the name of a business or university that needs someone with that skill, and at the same time inform a business about his or her availability. Businesses with export interests would know where to go to find qualified employees or consultants.

15. The Department of Education and the two major federal language teaching facilities should cooperate in developing textbook materials for classes beyond the first year for many of the less commonly taught languages. Foreign embassies probably would be willing to help in this.

16. While this book and most educational efforts are geared toward development of new language skills, greater attention must also be given to the retention of acquired or existing language skills.

17. The development of a key group of well-qualified translators and interpreters in all the major world languages should be an immediate priority of the federal government.

18. The National Institute of Education should research the dollars and cents value of the study of a foreign language to a student.

19. The Advertising Council of America should be enlisted to assist in a major public education program stressing the importance of foreign language study.

20. Special emphasis should be placed on training women in foreign language skills. Their average income and training remains appreciably below that of the average American male; yet their ranks among the employed have swelled from 18.4 million in 1950 to 40 million in 1977.

Business, Labor, and Foundation Leaders

1. A survey of the foreign languages taught in an area's elementary and high schools, and colleges should be prepared and publicized. If significant deficiencies are shown—and they are probable—business, labor, and educational leaders should plan together to rectify the situation.

2. Textbook publishers should prepare for more immersion education.

3. Job application forms should include a space to list knowledge of another language. Such information will be helpful in serving foreign visitors and potential customers, and a potential asset for export sales. It is a subtle way of letting people know that knowledge of a foreign language could be an asset in getting a job.

4. Business involved in international operations should establish overseas internships for college juniors and seniors and graduate students.

5. Publishers of bilingual books should be encouraged by foundations. Sasha Newborn of the Mudborn Press of California writes:

> As small publishers we are bending our efforts toward producing bilingual editions of poetry and prose, so that we can read better into other cultures, and perhaps understand our own better. . . . . Here is a suggestion, a tip from the Gulbenkian Foundation in Lisbon, Portugal: if money is available, let it buy books directly, to be distributed by the funding agency. Gulbenkian is supporting two bilingual Portuguese books for us this year—and it makes quite a difference.[5]

6. Magazine publishers should look into the profit-loss picture of magazines like *Reader's Digest* and other magazines that publish in other languages. *Scientific American,* for example, started a Chinese edition in January 1980, for circulation in the People's Republic of China. The first issue ran 25,000 copies. Magazines can add to their profitability by being more than monolingual.

7. More experimental marketing of foreign language cassettes should be provided for people to use when driving back and forth to work. The right packaging of a product could enrich what is now dead time for millions of commuters; and, at the same time, make money for some business(es).

8. The U.S. Chamber of Commerce and other business entities should follow the lead of the British Overseas Trade Board, which is actively promoting foreign language study among business executives and in educational institutions in Great Britain. They note that "a more positive attitude by industry and commerce towards foreign language skills would contribute significantly towards Britain's future success in overseas trade."[6]

Parents

1. Starting when children are young, parents should provide an opportunity for them to hear and learn other languages.

2. When moving, parents should check to see that the new school district offers foreign language courses. The simple process of asking is helpful, if nothing else, in embarrassing school officials who do not offer them!

3. Families can invite an exchange student to their homes, for a dinner with their family, or even for a semester or a school year.

Everyone

1. Organizations like the PTA, Rotary Club, League of Women Voters, labor unions, church, or synagogue can sponsor a survey of foreign language studies available in area schools and plan how to remedy deficiencies.

2. *No one should underestimate the power that a simple letter has.* If every member of Congress, every state legislator re-

ceived just ten letters from people in their districts, and every school board member received five, change would quickly result.

3. A letter to the editor of the local newspaper should be brief and to the point, describing action in behalf of the teaching of foreign language.

4. Anyone can suggest to a school board member, state legislator, member of Congress, or editor that he or she might get this book out of the library, or buy them a new book, or send a marked-up copy, asking that it be returned.

5. Friends may get together some evening to brainstorm on what could be done to help get things moving in the teaching of foreign languages in their community.

6. Foreign visitors should find signs in bus terminals, museums, and cultural centers that provide basic information in several other languages than English.

A story that grew out of the Korean War illustrates our situation. Marine General Lewis Puller and his men were trapped at the Chosin Reservoir when China entered the war and moved south. Puller is supposed to have said, "We've got the enemy on our right flank, on our left flank, in front of us, and behind us. They won't get away this time."[7]

That is an approximation of the position of those of us who believe that the study of foreign languages must forge ahead. Beleaguered by indifference and by unfavorable statistics, we must refuse to yield to pessimism. It is vital to the future of our nation, and to a world that must communicate that we do not surrender, but enter the fray with revived energy and determination. If we do that, we shall surprise ourselves. They won't get away this time.

Notes

Introduction

1. "Toward a National Foreign Language Policy," *Journal of Communication* 29, no. 2 (Spring 1979): 93–102.

2. "An Inward-Looking Nation," *New York Times,* 25 February 1978.

3. "A Memo to Secondary Schools, Students, and Parents," Stanford University Office of Admissions, October 1978.

4. "Shakeup in the City Schools Again," *Washington Post,* 6 September 1977.

5. Ooka, IX, quoted by Stanley J. Drazek and Henry A. Walker, "Survey of Senior Continuing Education/Extension Administrators," *National University Extension Association Spectator* 38, no. 16 (June 1974): 20–29.

Chapter 1

1. Quoted by Rose L. Hayden, Address to Utah School Administrator's Conference, 25 March 1977. Mimeographed, p. 13.

2. Reprint (Boston: Houghton Mifflin, 1943), pp. 419–420.

3. Modern Language Association and other groups, Task Force Report. Mimeographed, p. 1.

Chapter 2

1. "The State of Foreign Language Teaching," *Bulletin of the Association of Departments of Foreign Languages* 7, no. 1 (September 1975): 6.

2. Quoted by Loren Alexander, "Foreign Language Skills in Manufacturing Firms: Kansas, 1974," *Bulletin of the Association of Departments of Foreign Languages* 7, no. 2 (November 1975): 33.

3. Professor at Jackson State University. Statement to President's Commission on Foreign Language and International Studies, 13 April 1979.

4. Robert D. Buzzell, "Can You Standardize Multinational Marketing?" *Harvard Business Review* 96, no. 6 (November-December 1968): 102–113.

5. Thomas B. Macaulay, "On Mitford's History of Greece," *Knight's Quarterly,* no. 3 (November 1824).

6. "Summary of Recommendations," Task Force on Inflation, House

Budget Committee, 6 August 1979. Mimeographed, p. 11.

7. *Chicago Tribune,* 20 February 1975, p. 6 Section 7.

8. Jack Kolbert, Testimony to the President's Commission on Foreign Language and International Studies, 23 February 1979.

9. "Denmark's Quiet Giants," *Newsweek* (Pacific Edition), 5 May 1975, p. 46.

10. Erik J. Jansen to Val Hempel, 25 June 1975.

11. Paul Hirsch to Marquis Childs, 25 April 1979.

12. "Gauging a Family's Suitability for a Stint Overseas," *Business Week,* 16 April 1979, p. 130.

13. *Business America* 2, no. 13 (23 April 1979): inside cover.

14. Quoted by Rex M. Arnett, "Languages for the World of Work," *Bulletin of the Association of Departments of Foreign Languages* 7, no. 16 (May 1976): 16.

15. James C. Baker and John M. Ivanceivich, "The Assignment of American Executives Abroad: Systematic, Haphazard or Chaotic?" *California Management Review* 13, no. 3 (Spring 1971): 39–44.

16. Richard D. Lambert, *Language and Area Studies Review* (Philadelphia: American Academy of Political and Social Science, October 1973), pp. 52–53.

17. Anthony Paul, "Japan and the Falling Dollar," *Reader's Digest* 114, no. 681 (January 1979): 97f.

18. These illustrations are largely taken from *Crain's Chicago Business.*

19. David A. Ricks, Marilyn Y. C. Fu, and Jeffrey S. Arpan, *International Business Blunders* (Columbus, Ohio: Transemantics, 1974), p. 5.

20. Loren Alexander, "Foreign Language Skills in Manufacturing Firms: Kansas 1974," *Bulletin of the Association of Departments of Foreign Languages* 7, no. 2 (November 1975): 34. Quoted in part from an unpublished collection of seminar papers at Kansas State University written by Linda Bankes et al.

21. Edwin O. Reischauer, *Toward the 21st Century* (New York: Knopf, 1973), pp. 148–152.

22. *Expanding Consumer Goods Exports to Japan* (Tokyo: Japan Institute for Social and Economic Affairs and the Japan Federation of Economic Organizations, February 1979), pp. 3–7.

23. Address at symposium on "Preparing Tomorrow's Business Leaders Today," sponsored by the Graduate School of Business Administration, New York University, quoted in *Business and International Education: A Report Submitted by the Task Force on Business and International Education, Lee C. Nehrt, Chairman* (Washington: American Council on Education, 1977), p. 17.

24. "Escalating the Campaign Against Provincialism," *Bulletin of the Association of Departments of Foreign Languages,* 9, no. 1 (September 1977): 2.

25. Royal L. Tinsley, Jr., to Jimmy Carter, 15 September 1977.

26. 12 December 1978.

194 · NOTES

27. *Business and International Education: A Report Submitted by the Task Force on Business and International Education, Lee C. Nehrt, Chairman* (Washington: American Council on Education, 1977).

28. Don Arnold, Robert Morgenroth, and William Morgenroth, *Business and International Education,* Ibid., p. 52.

29. Michael J. McManus, "Now Is the Time for Foreign Trade," *New Haven* (Conn.) *Register,* 14 January 1979.

30. "Survey of International Education in Houston," folder published by the Education Task Force, International Business Committee, Houston Chamber of Commerce, July 1977.

Chapter 3

1. Memorandum to Paul Simon, 23 February 1978.

2. Speech, University of Chicago, 22 May 1979.

3. *Education for Global Independence* (Washington: American Council on Education, 1975), p. 3.

4. *Washington Star,* 18 February 1979.

5. Memorandum for the President's Commission on Foreign Languages and International Studies, 1979.

6. *Benton* (Illinois) *Evening News,* 15 January 1979.

7. "Institute Established for Advanced Russian Studies," *Bulletin of the Association of Departments of Foreign Languages* 7, no. 2 (November 1975): 43.

8. Royal L. Tinsley, Jr., to Jimmy Carter, 15 September 1977.

9. Thomas Bailey, *A Diplomatic History of the American People,* 9th edition (New York: F. S. Crofts & Co., 1940), p. 3.

10. Statement by Rose L. Hayden to the House Subcommittee on International Security and Scientific Affairs, 22 March 1978.

11. John Wilson Lewis, Stanford University, memorandum to Paul Simon, 23 February 1978.

12. Timothy S. Healy, S.J., president, Georgetown University, "Language and Civilization," *Language in American Life* (Washington: Georgetown University Press, 1978), p. 8.

13. Elizabeth Lubin, "American Military and Japanese Municipality at the Interface of Culture: Official Relations Between U.S. Bases and Local Communities in Japan" unpublished thesis, Harvard University, April 1979), pp. 55–62.

14. *Ibid.*

15. Sue E. Berryman et al., *Foreign Language and International Studies Specialists: The Marketplace and National Policy* (Santa Monica, CA.: Rand Corporation, 1979), p. 96.

16. Frequently quoted statement that may or may not be authentic. Charles V was born in 1500, died in 1558.

17. Morton Kondracke, "The Ugly American Redux," *New Republic* 180, no. 13 (31 March 1979): 12–15.

18. While a U.S. delegate to the United Nations' Special Session on Disarmament during the early summer of 1978, I invited the Vietnamese delegation to have lunch with me. They indicated they first wanted to contact Hanoi. A few days later we had our lunch—attended also by Representative William Lehman of Florida and a representative of the State Department. The Vietnamese indicated for the first time that they were willing and eager to have full diplomatic and trade ties with the United States and that they were willing to forget what up to that point had been a stumbling block to such relations: a commitment they felt they had from President Richard Nixon for $3 billion in aid after the war. This luncheon message was immediately relayed to Washington. I asked the Vietnamese if they would like to come to Washington to pursue the discussions further, and they set up two qualifications: First, they would have to clear it with Hanoi, and second, I would have to get permission from Washington since they are restricted by the United States to staying within twenty-five miles of the United Nations. Both Hanoi and Washington approved, and a dinner meeting was held at my home with two Vietnamese officials, a few members of the House and Senate, and two representatives of the State Department. All of us came away with the feeling that the time had arrived to reconcile our differences and move ahead. Unfortunately, officials at top levels of the State Department and the White House felt it would be politically imprudent to do so.

19. Royal L. Tinsley, Jr., to Jimmy Carter, 15 September 1977.

20. *New York Times,* 2 February 1979, p. A24.

21. Address in Raleigh, North Carolina, 2 April 1979.

22. *National Needs for International Education* (Washington: Georgetown University Center for Strategic and International Studies, February 1977), pp. 2–3.

23. "Foreign Language and International Education," *Communicator* 9, no. 8 (April 1979): 1.

Chapter 4

1. *Great Books* edition (Chicago: Encyclopaedia Britannica, 1952), Volume II, p. 300.

2. "Bribing Colleges with Tax Dollars," 18 March 1979.

3. Address at the dedication of the National Humanities Center, Research Triangle Park, North Carolina, 7 April 1979.

4. Statement to President's Commission on Foreign Language and International Studies, 1979, Mimeographed, p. 4.

5. Jay Matthews, "Easy as ABC?" 18 April 1979.

6. Robert Louis Stevenson, "Foreign Children," *A Child's Garden of Verses* (New York: J. H. Sears & Co., 1926), p. 24.

7. Address in Houston, Texas, 7 March 1979.

8. Mark Twain, *The Adventures of Huckleberry Finn,* Centennial Edition (New York: Harper & Row, 1978), pp. 110–111.

9. Edwin O. Reischauer, *Toward the 21st Century* (New York: Knopf, 1973), p. 151.

10. Henri Peyre, quoted by Elona Vaisnys, Statement to the President's Commission on Foreign Language and International Studies, December 1978.

11. Often quoted, but source for it uncertain.

12. "An Inward-Looking Nation," *New York Times,* 25 February 1978.

13. Reischauer, *Toward the 21st Century,* pp. 180–181.

14. Raphael G. Alberola, president, Berlitz, Statement to the President's Commission on Foreign Language and International Studies, 12 January 1979.

15. Richard Brod to Paul simon, 16 October 1979.

16. Interview with Paul Simon, 18 January 1979.

17. Quoted by Senator Mark O. Hatfield, written statement to President's Commission on Foreign Language and International Studies, n.d.

18. David Vidal, "New Transit Police Drill: Spanish," *New York Times,* 2 July 1979, p. 1.

19. Rose L. Hayden, "In the National Interest," *Bulletin of the Association of Departments of Foreign Languages* 6, no. 3 (March 1975): 13.

20. Jane O'Reilly, "Thumbs Up for the U.S.A.," *Time,* 20 August 1979, p. 74.

21. Robert E. Ward, *National Needs for International Education* (Washington: Georgetown University Center for Strategic and International Studies, 1977), p. 4.

22. Survey conducted in April 1979 for President's Commission on Foreign Language and International Studies, funded by U.S. Office of Education, Ford Foundation, Hewlett Foundation, Joint National Committee for Languages, and Modern Language Association.

23. From "Maxims for Revolutionists," in *Man and Superman* (London: Westminster, 1903), pp. 225–244.

24. Howard Fabing, *Fischerisms* (Cincinnati: University of Cincinnati Medical College Bookstore, 1930), p. 17.

25. *Education for Global Independence* (Washington: American Council on Education, 1975), p. 5.

26. James D. Anderson, "Ad Hoc and Selective Translations of Scientific and Technical Journal Articles," *Journal of the American Society for Information Science* 29, no. 3 (May 1978): 130.

27. Betty Brociner Bogart, "National Translations Center," *Translation News* 8, no. 2 (December 1978): 13.

Chapter 5

1. Thomas Jefferson to J. W. Eppes, 28 July 1787.

2. *De pueris statim ac liberaliter instituendis,* Opera I of Opera Omnia, 10 volumes published 1703–1706 (London: Greg Reprint, 1960), p. 317.

3. Pamela M. Martin, Embassy of the United Republic of Cameroon, to Paul Simon, 23 March 1979.

4. People's Republic of China. The Republic of China is listed as Taiwan.

5. Reg and Dena Leighton, "Should Children Learn a Foreign Language?" *Australian Women's Weekly,* 7 March 1979.

6. Theodore Roosevelt, letter read at the All-American Festival, New York [January 5, 1919], cited in *Familiar Quotations,* John Bartlett (New York: Little, Brown & Co., 1955), p. 780.

7. *The American High School Today* (New York: McGraw-Hill, 1959), p. 72. One respected dissenter from that generally accepted theory is Professor James J. Asher of San Jose State University. He believes that children learn more rapidly only because they combine the learning process with action, while older children and adults tend to learn a language in a more sedentary style and, therefore, more slowly.

8. Militating against a Quebec-type separation in the United States is the fact that, with the exception of Puerto Rico, the Hispanic population of the United States is scattered in every state in the union and is gradually being assimilated, just as every other immigrant group has been. Like other immigrant groups, there are concentrated pockets, particularly in larger cities, but as their education and income levels go up, they leave that language concentration community for the suburbs and other places in the nation.

9. Immersion is discussed in more detail in Chapter 7.

10. *Foreign Language Teaching in Illinois: Report of the Foreign Language Study Group* (Carbondale, Ill.: Southern Illinois University, 1957), p. 15.

11. *Northwestern Newsletter for Secondary School Counselors,* n.d., apparently issued during the 1978–79 school year.

12. Jody Beck, "Dixon Kids Switching Schools," *Washington Star,* 9 September 1979.

13. Daniel A. Salmon, "The School of International Studies: Interdisciplinary Education at the High School Level," *Career Education,* date and number unknown.

14. Doug McMillan, "School Board Ups Graduation Loan," *Nevada State Journal,* 4 March 1979.

15. E. F. Timpe, "The Effect of Foreign Language Study on ACT Scores," paper submitted to Richard Brod of the Modern Language Association, 1979.

16. *Wall Street Journal,* 15 February 1978.

17. Albert W. JeKenta and Percy Fearing, "Current Trends in Curriculum: Elementary and Secondary Schools," quoting from a dissertation by Kathryn Talley, *Britannica Review of Foreign Language Education* (Chicago: Encyclopaedia Britannica, 1968), p. 143.

18. E. Jules Mandel, project director, to President's Commission on Foreign Language and International Studies, 23 February 1979.

19. *Wampeters, Foma, and Grand Falloons* (New York: Dell, 1976), p. 276.

20. *Nordwest Zeitung,* 28 April 1979.

21. *The Foreign Language Attainments of Language Majors in the Senior Year: A Survey Conducted in U.S. Colleges and Universities,* compiled by the Laboratory for Research in Instruction, Graduate School of Education, Harvard University (Cambridge, Mass.: Harvard University Printing Office, 1967), p. 202.

22. Mrs. R. Loch to Paul Simon, 6 March 1979.

23. *Toward the 21st Century* (New York: Knopf, 1973), pp. 190–191.

Chapter 6

1. Speech at the University of Massachusetts, Amherst, 17 May 1973.

2. Speech in Liverpool on "Scientific Education," n.d.

3. *The American High School Today* (New York: McGraw-Hill, 1959), p. 4.

4. James E. Alatis et al., *Foreign Languages and Linguistics Academic Program Review* (Tallahassee: State University System of Florida, 1978), p. 90.

5. Faculty of Arts and Sciences, *Report on the Core Curriculum* (Cambridge, Mass.: Harvard University, 15 February 1978), p. 4.

6. William H. Trombley, "Building Enrollments: It Pays to Advertise," *Change* 10, no. 1 (January 1978): 34.

7. *Foreign Language Attainments of Language Majors in the Senior Year: A Survey Conducted in U.S. Colleges and Universities,* compiled by the Laboratory for Research in Instruction, Graduate School of Education, Harvard University (Cambridge, Mass.: Harvard University Printing Office, 1967).

8. Statement to the President's Commission on Foreign Language and International Studies, Raleigh, North Carolina, 13 April 1979.

9. Quoted by Barbara B. Burn, "Higher Education and Global Perspectives," a report for the Carnegie Council on Policy Studies in Higher Education, November 1977. Mimeographed, p. 36.

10. "The Language of Survival: Find a Need and Fill It," *Change* 10, no. 1 (January 1978): 36–37.

11. John E. D'Andrea and foreign language faculty members to Paul Simon, 2 March 1979.

12. Conversation with Paul Simon, 4 November 1979.

13. Statement to the President's Commission on Foreign Language and International Studies, New York City, 11 January 1979.

14. Louise J. Hubbard, "The Minority Student in the Foreign Language Field," paper prepared for the President's Commission on Foreign Language and International Studies, 1979.

15. Joseph J. Rodgers, "A Case Study for the Study of Languages in Black Colleges—A Position Paper," Lincoln University, Pennsylvania.

16. Hugh M. Jenkins, statement for the President's Commission on

Foreign Language and International Studies, March 1979.

17. Wallace B. Edgerton, statement for the President's Commission on Foreign Language and International Studies, New York City, 11 January 1979.

18. Sharon Conway, "A Language Barrier," *Washington Post,* 14 May 1979.

19. Peter I. Rose, "The Senior Fulbright-Hays Program in East Asia and the Pacific," *Exchange* 12, no. 2 (Fall 1976): 22.

20. Jerald C. Brauer, University of Chicago, "Impressions," a report to the Swedish Consul General in Chicago, 7 June 1979. Mimeographed.

21. 1787 law, quoted by Rose L. Hayden, Address to Utah School Administrator's Conference, 25 March 1977. Mimeographed, p. 12.

22. The National Association of State Universities and Land-Grant Colleges, statement to the President's Commission on Foreign Language and International Studies, 10 May 1979.

23. Burn, "Higher Education and Global Perspectives," pp. 7–8.

24. Barbara B. Burn, *International Education: New Needs and Definitions* (to be published by Jossey-Bass, San Francisco), p. 119 of manuscript.

25. *Ibid,* p. 106.

26. Letter forwarded by Chancellor William P. Gerberding to Paul Simon, 13 March 1979.

27. Richard D. Lambert, *Language and Area Studies Review* (Philadelphia: American Academy of Political and Social Science, October 1973), p. 394.

28. Rose L. Hayden, testimony to House Subcommittee on International Security and International Affairs, 22 March 1978.

29. Statement to the President's Commission on Foreign Language and International Studies, January 1979.

30. *National Needs for International Education* (Washington: Georgetown University Center for Strategic and International Studies, 1977), p. 4.

Chapter 7

1. *Thorough Method vs. Natural Method: A Letter to Dr. L. Sauveur* (Boston, 1878), p. 16.

2. "The State of Foreign Language Teaching," *Bulletin of the Association of Departments of Foreign Languages* 7, no. 1 (September 1975): 6. Peyre, professor emeritus and former chairman of the Department of Romance Languages at Yale University, is now executive officer of the Program in French at City University of New York.

3. *The Foreign Language Attainments of Language Majors in the Senior Year: A Survey Conducted in U.S. Colleges and Universities,* compiled by the Laboratory for Research in Instruction, Graduate School of Education, Harvard University (Cambridge, Mass.: Harvard University Printing Office, 1967), p. 201.

4. Barbara B. Burn, *International Education: New Needs and Definitions* (to be published by Jossey-Bass, San Francisco), p. 66 of manuscript.

5. H. A. Merklein, "Multinational Corporate Perceptions of an International M.B.A. Degree," *Bulletin of the Association of Departments of Foreign Languages* 6, no. 4 (May 1975): 34.

6. George S. Springsteen, statement to the President's Commission on Foreign Language and International Studies, 26 October 1978.

7. Louis G. Kelly, *25 Centuries of Language Teaching* (Rowley, Mass.: Newbury House, 1969), pp. 283–284.

8. Sue E. Berryman et al., *Foreign Language and International Studies Specialists: The Marketplace and National Policy* (Santa Monica, Calif.: Rand Corporation, 1979), p. 173.

9. Burn, *International Education: New Needs and Definitions,* p. 66 of manuscript.

10. "Second Language Spoken Here," *Christian Science Monitor,* 15 January 1979.

11. Statement to President's Commission for Foreign Language and International Studies, 21 February 1979.

12. John Rassias to Barbara B. Burn, 10 December 1978.

13. Kelly, *25 Centuries of Language Teaching,* p. 99.

14. *Colloquiorum liber,* from Opera Omnia, published 1703–1706 (London: Greg Reprint, 1960), p. 629.

15. Cynthia Parsons, "She Makes English a Parallel Language," *Christian Science Monitor,* 15 January 1979.

16. "The Participatory Classroom," *Change* 10, no. 1 (January 1978): 47.

17. Peggy Thomson, "The Rest of the World is *Fou,*" *American Education* 14, no. 9 (November 1978): 30.

18. *Ibid,* p. 31.

19. Draft report, n.d., p. 27.

20. Dale L. Lange, ed., "Implications of Psychological Research for Second Language Learning," *Foreign Language Education: A Reappraisal* (Skokie, Ill.: National Textbook, 1972), p. 158.

21. *Chicago Tribune,* 26 August 1979.

22. "Takoma Park Cluster Schools," folder published by the Montgomery County (Maryland) Public Schools, n.d., pp. 7–8.

23. Leon I. Twarog, "Beyond Survival: The Role of FL Programs in the High Schools and Two-Year Colleges," *Profession '77* (New York: Modern Language Association, 1977), p. 52.

24. Cynthia Parsons, "Warning on Study Abroad: Beward the Superficial," *Christian Science Monitor,* 5 February 1979.

25. Stan Luxenberg, "All the Class a Stage," *Change,* 10, no. 1 (January 1978): 33.

26. *Foreign Language Teaching in Illinois: Report of the Foreign Language Study Group* (Carbondale, Ill.: Southern Illinois University, 1957), p. 27.

27. Bertil Ostergren, quoted by Francis X. Sutton, F. Champion Ward, and James A. Perkins, *Internationalizing Higher Education: A United States Approach* (New York: International Council for Educational Development, 1974), pp. 45–46.

28. James A. Alatis et al., *Foreign Language and Linguistics Academic Program Review* (Tallahassee: State University System of Florida, 1978), p. 64.

29. Walter B. Mullane to Paul Simon, 30 April 1979.

30. Thomas B. Macaulay to Macvey Napier, 26 November 1836.

31. Richard D. Lambert, *Language and Area Studies Review* (Philadelphia: American Academy of Political and Social Science, October 1973), pp. 58–59.

Chapter 8

1. "A National Foreign Language Program for the 1970's," statement issued by the Modern Language Association, the American Council on the Teaching of Foreign Languages, and other groups, 1973.

2. A history of the Berlitz organization issued by the company in 1978, their one-hundredth anniversary year. Mimeographed.

3. R. Ascham, *The Scholemaster, Book II,* in *The Whole Works,* vol. III (London: John Russell Smith, 1864), p. 210.

4. Statement to the President's Commission on Foreign Language and International Studies, 12 January 1979.

5. *Ibid.*

6. Cheryl M. Fields, "How Berlitz Taught Me Spanish Rapidamente," *Chronicle of Higher Education,* 17 July 1978, p. 4, and 24 July 1979, p. 6.

7. Statement issued by the Modern Language Association, the American Council on the Teaching of Foreign Languages, and other groups.

8. R. E. Moore, "Radio Instruction in Languages," *Modern Language Journal* 16, no. 3 (December 1931): 213.

9. William S. Paley to Luis A. Garcia, 1 November 1950.

10. William Barnes and John Heath Morgan, *The Foreign Service of the United States* (Westport, Conn.: Greenwood Press, 1961), p. 139.

Chapter 9

1. "Internationalizing Public Education: What the States Are Doing," *Exchange* 12, no. 2 (Fall 1976): 3–8.

2. Memorandum to James Perkins, chairman, President's Commission on Foreign Language and International Studies, 12 April 1979.

3. Lorraine A. Strasheim, "Foreign Languages in the 'Average' School Situation: Reaching Toward the 21st Century," prepared for the President's Commission on Foreign Language and International Studies, 12 December 1978. Mimeographed, p. 6.

4. *Ibid.,* p. 7.

5. Rose Hayden, "Statewide Approaches to Change in International/

Intercultural Education," compiled for the American Council on Education, August 1975. Mimeographed, p. 118.

6. *Ibid.,* p. 111.

7. Betty Bullard, conversation with Paul Simon, 4 October 1979.

8. "North Carolina Position Statement on Foreign Language Education," 1979. Mimeographed.

9. Hayden, "Statewide Approaches to Change in International/ Intercultural Education," p. 77.

10. John Pope, "Can a State Learn French? Mais Oui, a Louisianan Believes," *Washington Post,* 7 November 1979.

11. Conversation with Paul Simon, 4 October 1979.

12. Richard D. Lambert, *Language and Area Studies Review* (Philadelphia: American Academy of Political and Social Science, October 1973), pp. 41–42.

13. Charles B. Neff, memorandum to James Perkins, chairman, President's Commission on Foreign Language and International Studies, 12 April 1979.

Chapter 10

1. "Tongue-Tied Americans," *New York Times,* 24 March 1978, p. A26.

2. "The Current Need: More Jobs, Fewer Job Seekers," *Bulletin of the Association of Departments of Foreign Languages* 9, no. 1 (September 1977): 19.

3. James L. Oswald to Paul Simon, 25 March 1979.

4. William J. Ransbottom to Paul Simon, 19 March 1979.

5. Dennis A. Leventhal to Paul Simon, 7 March 1979.

6. Some months after receiving this letter I tried phoning the writer, Dennis A Leventhal, to see if anything had developed for him, and the operator told me the phone was no longer in service. I assumed that he might have employment, and a letter to him brought this response: "I have accepted a position as a China Project Coordinator with the American Cyanamid Company, headquartered in Wayne, New Jersey. The avenues for career development here look rather interesting."

7. Lewis Grossberger, "The Ph.D. Job Hunt Is a Losing Game," *Washington Post,* 30 December 1978.

8. "Survey of Ph.D. Job Market in Foreign Languages," *Bulletin of the Association of Departments of Foreign Languages* 6, no. 1 (September 1974): 18.

9. Barbara B. Burn, *International Education: New Needs and Definitions* (to be published by Jossey-Bass, San Francisco), p. 27 of manuscript.

10. Claus Reschke, "Career Education at the College Level: A Modest Proposal," *Bulletin of the Association of Departments of Foreign Languages* 9, no. 1 (September 1977): 44.

11. Statement for President's Commission on Foreign Language and International Studies, 30 March 1979.

12. Statement for President's Commission on Foreign Language and International Studies, n.d.

13. Mike Granberry, "Woes of Latins Exemplified by Moret Tragedy," Los Angeles Times News Service in the 29 July 1979 *Washington Post.*

14. M. Rex Arnett, "Languages for the World of Work," *Bulletin of the Association of Departments of Foreign Languages* 7, no. 16 (May 1976): 16. Survey by Olympus Research Corporation.

15. "Thumbs Up for the U.S.A.," *Time,* 20 August 1979, p. 73.

16. William F. Donny, *Postgraduate Activities: All Degree Levels in Pennsylvania, 1978* (Harrisburg, Pa.: Pennsylvania Department of Education, 1979), pp. 3–52.

17. Lane Jennings, "Unmaking Our Own Job Crises," *Bulletin of the Association of Departments of Foreign Languages* 6, no. 4 (May 1975): 14.

18. Quoted by Philip M. Knox, Jr., vice-president, Sears, Roebuck and Co., to Paul Simon, 25 June 1979.

19. John Dillon, "Millhiser Muses from Corporate Peak," *Richmond Times-Dispatch* 5 February 1979, p. A7.

20. Howard Van Zandt to Paul Simon, 19 March 1979.

21. *Columbus* (Ohio) *Citizen-Journal,* 18 November 1978.

22. Y. W. Bator, statement to President's Commission on Foreign Language and International Studies, 12 January 1979.

23. Michael Wines, "As More Companies Send Men to Foreign Lands, Language Schools Thrive—and Help Solve Problems," *Wall Street Journal,* 20 August 1973.

24. *Ibid.*

25. Robert Masello, "In Other Words," *New York Times,* 3 September 1979, p. 76.

26. *Business and International Education: A Report Submitted by the Task Force on Business and International Education to the American Council on Education* (Washington: American Council on Education, 1975), p. 14.

Chapter 11

1. Part of formal declaration of National Foreign Language Week for 1979.

2. Also named to the commission, in addition to me, were Carol Baumann, formerly at the University of Wisconsin and now with the State Department; Ernest Boyer, then Commissioner of Education and now president of the Carnegie Foundation for the Advancement of Teaching; Priscilla Ching-Chung, visiting scholar at the University of Hawaii; Betty Bullard, education director of the Asia Society; Rep. Millicent Fenwick; Wayne Fredericks, government affairs director of the international operations of the Ford Motor Company; Edmund Gleazer, Jr., president of the American Association of Community and Junior Colleges; Senator Mark

Hatfield; Rev. Timothy Healy, S.J., president of Georgetown University; Fred Hechinger, president of the New York Times Foundation; Vivian Horner, vice-president, Educational and Children's Programming, Warner Cable Corporation; Allen Kassof, former Princeton dean and director of the International Research and Exchange Board; Consuelo Nieto, assistant professor at California State University; John Rassias, professor at Dartmouth; Edwin O. Reischauer, former Ambassador to Japan and Harvard professor; Elona Vaisnys, a Lithuanian specialist and vice-president of the Association for the Advancement of the Baltic States; Sam Myers, executive director, National Association for Equal Opportunity in Higher Education; Robert Ward, director of the Center for Research and International Studies, Stanford University; J. F. Otero, international vice-president of the Brotherhood of Railway and Airline Clerks; Rep. Leon Panetta of California; John Reinhardt, director of the International Communication Agency; Sarah Deben, development representative of the Florida Department of Commerce; Samuel Stapleton, former director of the Defense Language Institute and now a personnel consultant. Special credit for helping to create the commission should go to three members of my staff: Dwight Mason, now with the State Department; David Solomon, now a Harvard law student; and Vicki Otten, still a member of my staff.

3. Copies of the report are available from the Government Printing Office, Washington, D.C. 20401, for $4.75.

Chapter 12

1. "A Frame of Reference for Federal Interest in International Studies," Mimeographed.

2. Robert Adams and Corinne Shelling, eds. *Corners of a Foreign Field*, (New York: Rockefeller Foundation, 1979), p. 107.

3. Myrian Met to Paul Simon, 9 March 1979.

4. Albert Shanker, president of the American Federation of Teachers, calls our present language situation "a national crisis" and suggests that schools

> can start with the teachers. Teachers are role models for students. If they are studying languages—in programs taught by their colleagues, the language teachers—students will catch on that this is important. Teachers now get salary credit for additional courses they take. Language courses, given right in their own or nearby schools, should be eligible for such credit.

Albert Shanker, "We Need to Learn Foreign Languages," *New York Times*, 24 June 1979.

5. Sasha Newborn to Paul Simon, 4 March 1979.

6. "Foreign Languages for Overseas Trade," a folder published by the British Overseas Trade Board, May 1979.

7. Edwin McDowell, "Beset on All Sides, Detroit Still Exudes Confidence," *New York Times*, 5 August 1979, p. F9.

Index